Postnational democracy

The European Union in search

of a political philosophy

Deirdre M. Curtin

This is a revised and expanded version of the Inaugural
Lecture pronounced by Dr. Deirdre M. Curtin on accepting
the Chair of the Law of International Organisations,
University of Utrecht, the Netherlands.

KLUWER LAW
INTERNATIONAL
THE HAGUE · LONDON · BOSTON

Published by Kluwer Law International
P.O. Box 85889
2508 CN The Hague, The Netherlands

Sold and distributed in the USA and Canada by
Kluwer Law International
675 Massachusetts Avenue
Cambridge, MA 02139, USA

Sold and distributed in all other countries by
Kluwer Law International
Distribution Centre
P.O. Box 322
3300 AH Dordrecht, The Netherlands

A C.I.P. Catalogue record for this book is available from the Library of Congress

02-0700-250 ts

Photograph cover: From: 'The Utrecht Psalter in Medieval Art' ISBN 90-6194-328-0, with permission of Museum Catherijn Convent, University Library, Ms. 32 (Utrecht Psalter). F. 90 v . (Illustration to the Creed 'Fides Catholicam' - Asthamarian Creed). Representation of a conciliar meeting.

Printed on acid-free paper

Cover design: Robert Vulkers

ISBN 90 411 0447 X

Kluwer Law International incorporates the publishing programmes of Graham & Trotman Ltd, Kluwer Law and Taxation Publishers and Martinus Nijhoff Publishers

Postnational
democracy

'... on the eve of the 40th anniversary of the signing of the Treaties of Rome. If we were thinking of that anniversary in human terms it could coincide with a mid-life crisis. And, given the organic development of the European project, perhaps we should recognise the potential analogy. A key element, after all, has been that capacity for organic growth. And yet, having the capacity for such development does not guarantee that it will happen or that it will continue. There must be a dynamic which triggers it from within.'

(Mary Robinson, President of Ireland,
Utrecht, 18 March 1997).

POSTNATIONAL DEMOCRACY

THE EUROPEAN UNION IN SEARCH OF A POLITICAL PHILOSOPHY

1. Introduction

In 1669 Sir Isaac Newton was appointed Lucasian Professor of Mathematics in Cambridge. For Newton true space was absolute, always similar and immovable.[1] This was a revolutionary way of thinking in its time, replacing the holistic medieval conception of the world as a living organism. In the intervening centuries Newton's formulation of the mathematical laws of physical space was laid out, clarified, and perfected. By the 20th century this vision of the universe was reduced to common knowledge that formed a key part of the background understanding we all had come to accept. William Blake, the English poet, famously captured this understanding in verse as 'single vision and Newtons sleep'.[2] The limits of single vision, or one point perspective as others might term it, were ever more exposed as the years advanced. By the last decades of the 20th century another Lucasian Professor of Mathematics had begun to get to grips with the implications of these limits of the accepted model. Stephen Hawking, now occupying Newton's old Cambridge chair localised the applications of what Newton and we thought was natural and necessary and in so doing exposed us to fragmentation and indeterminacy.[3] Now we are left to labour with the hints that have been exposed of the directions in which we must move on.

In the decades immediately prior to Newton's transformative period in Cambridge, the social world too was being turned upside down. The Peace of Westphalia of 1648 announced the dawn of the European (nation) state and a new system of spatial organisation that was founded

---

1.　See further, E.N. da C. Andrade, *Sir Isaac Newton* (London, 1954).

2.　Quoted by R.B.J. Walker, *Inside/Outside: International Relations as Political Theory* (Cambridge, 1993), p. 129.

3.　See, in particular, S. Hawking, *The Nature of Space and Time* (Princeton, 1996).

in the naturalness of state sovereignty. The principle of the territorial state implied by state sovereignty constituted a revolution in terms of the unifying and dividing of the preexisting patchwork political communities in medieval Europe.[4] During the ensuing centuries both the internal and the external orders of the nation-state were laid out, clarified and perfected in Europe. The state came to be regarded as the organisation with a legitimate monopoly of official violence and the capacity to carry out acts of governance or control exclusively within its own territory.[5] Moreover, the legitimacy of the modern nation-state came to depend in the final instance on the claim that it and it alone is able to allow the citizens of particular states to participate in a broader humanity. The conventional wisdom of Western political thought can then be told as a tale in which reason, history, property, nation, and, not least, democracy have featured as prominent heros. The conventional history of international relations, by contrast, is told as a tale of tragedy and power politics.

Like the case of physics, our shared understandings as to the nature and location of political community are firmly rooted in the system which evolved after the Treaty of Westphalia. As we approach the tail end of this Millenium the limits of our shared understandings are increasingly exposed. Our century has seen failure, reconsideration and initial efforts at a new organisation of space that may be epitomized by the European Community (EC)/European Union (EU). The EC as it was originally conceived and implemented over the course of the years was a novelty, a completely new social order, a new idea. In the words of one eminent commentator:

'the young European Community had something of the historical and philosophical significance of the young United States of America or the France of 1789 or the young Soviet Union under Lenin'.[6]

Today, sadly, this historical and philosophical significance, has receded into the background (quite apart from the fact that the examples were not

---

4. See further, J. Ruggie, 'Territoriality and Beyond: Problematising Modernity in International Relations', 47 *International Organisation* (1993), p. 139. See however, M. Fischer, 'Feudal Europe, 800-1300: Communal Discourse and Conflictual Practices' 46 *International Organisation* (1992), p. 427. See also, J. Strayer, *On the Medieval Origins of the Modern State*, (Princeton, 1970).

5. See, M. Weber, *Economy and Society*, Vol. 2, (original edition, 1922).

6. P. Allott, 'The European Community is not the true European Community' 100 Yale L. J. (1991), pp. 2485, 2494.

necessarily propitious). We have only the barest hints of success; the European Union as it has more recently become, is stalled and deeply troubled.

The philosophical potential of the Union lies in its challenge to the understanding of the state as the only possible locus of political community and thus of political identity. This may seem a rather facile statement: after all who thinks of the EU, no matter how sophisticated it may be as a model of integration or as an international organisation, in terms of political identity? Those who do recognise this potential are defeated by the effort to explain it: we are left with generalisations such as that the European Union is the most ambitious political project of this century or the negative formulation of Jacques Delors that it constitutes 'an unidentified political object'.[7] Such categorisations are of course not very helpful in terms of explaining what the problem is as we approach the Third Millenium and how a reconceptualisation of the European Union might well be part of the solution.

It seems in any event clear that the European Union *can* only become a conceivable or identifiable political object at the price of a considerable effort of re-imagination or re-conceiving of fundamental 'shared understandings'. Just as the centuries have exposed the limits of the inertial frame of reference ('ether') on which Newtonian physics were once thought to depend, the exercise I propose to you involves some reconceptualisation of the inertial frame of reference of the nation-state in Europe. We are left to labour with hints that have been exposed of the directions in which progress may well lie. I use the term 'progress' advisedly. It refers to the contemporary scenario where decision-making in the European Union concerns, according to some calculations, 80% of policy areas falling previously within the remit of national governments and parliaments. It refers to the fact that among those policy areas, we are no longer just talking about socio-economic or environmental matters; we are talking also about immigration, policing and criminal law, to mention what many would regard as the 'inner core' of national sovereignty. And we are talking about decision-making which takes place in such a manner that it increasingly recalls what Hannah Arendt, in a different context, famously termed the authoritarian temptation.[8]

The conclusion is that there is a terrible 'here and now'. The question we must now ask is where can we possibly *go* with this 'here' as our starting point? Surely any 'there' in the sense of a different destination risks being an even more unattractive 'fuite en avant'? Many

---

7. See, P. Thibaud, 'L'Europe, Essai d'Identification', *Esprit*, Nov. 1991, p. 47.

8. See, H. Meijers, 'European Cooperation: An Authoritarian Temptation?', *Fortress Europe?*, No. 49, December 1996/January 1997, p. 12.

are those who conclude that the safest and best option is simply to retreat to what we are familar with, even if its imperfection is acknowledged, the nation-state. The nation-state as the true and only possible locus of democratic politics. Isn't the nation-state after all the only conceivable political roof for national culture?

The task of reconceptualisation may appear to many an innately unappealing exercise: better to stay with what we know and what has been consolidated over the course of many centuries, often by dint of war or revolution, than to risk throwing the baby out with the bath water. But the task need *not* be an impossible one and certainly is not to be equated with total destruction. On the contrary it may sooner be equated with survival in the modern world in which the whole concept of geographical borders is rapidly becoming irrelevant. Just think of how global computer-based communications cut across territorial borders, creating a new realm of human activity and undermining the feasability -and legitimacy- of applying laws based on geographic boundaries to this new sphere. While these electronic communications play havoc with geographic boundaries, a *new boundary*, made up of screens and passwords that separate the world of atoms from the world of bits is emerging.[9] The new problems are shifting old perspectives and opening up new perspectives for the future. History has indeed become mobilised.[10] As the Nobel prize winning Irish poet *Seamus Heaney* elegantly put it in verse:

'Whatever is given/can always be reimagined, however four-square/ ... it happens to be'[11]

In order to arrive at the requisite effort of reimagination a process of disentanglement or separation is required. To separate does not mean to repudiate; it means to step back in order to rethink some of the prevailing ideas and images that have shaped the political understanding of most modern citizens in Western Europe.[12] What require separation are a

---

9.   See, D. Johnson and D. Post, 'Law and Borders - The Rise of Law in Cyberspace', unpublished manuscript.

10.   See, J. Habermas, 'Citizenship and National Identity: Some Reflections on the Future of Europe', 12 *Praxis International* (1992), p. 1.

11.   S. Heaney, 'Frontiers of Writing' in *The Redress of Poetry* (London, 1995), p. 200. Quoted in R. Kearney, *Postnationalist Ireland. Politics, Culture, Philosophy* (London, 1997).

12.   See, R. Kearney, ibid. at p. 1.

number of elided terms which have conditioned our political culture: in particular, state and nation, nationality, culture and political identity, democracy and sovereignty. The purpose of the exercise is not to make a 'bonfire of the certainties' but rather to reimagine different variables. The term 'postnational democracy' is meant to express not only the separation from the 'here and now' in the nation-state but it also implies a more formative notion of politics than that implied by liberal political philosophy. Rather than stressing the fact that the journey is to an unknown destination[13] it is the *transcendental capacity* which is paramount.

The departure point of the voyage is in any event clear: it is where we are *now*. So I don't share the wisdom of my countryman who when asked by a fellow traveller along a road for directions as to how to get to 'there', a particular place, replies as a witty and willy Celt to the effect that he should avoid starting from 'here'![14] My view is that we start from 'here' but at the critical juncture where a serious re-evaluation of our 'shared understandings' has to take place. Moreover the 'there' we may ultimately arrive at may prove to have more in common with the system that prevailed *before* the territorial state and *before* the principle of state sovereignty was conceived: the so-called 'return of the Middle Ages'.[15] The political *reorganisation* of European space must build on the history of European modernity (post-Westphalia, post-Newton) but go beyond the now exposed limits of the nation-state and the principle of national sovereignty.

In secular terms the location of political community only knows the historical precedents in Europe of city-states, nation-states and Empires.[16] This paper starts with a brief historical exegesis into the

---

13. See, A. Schonfeld, *Europe: Journey to an Unknown Destination* (Middlesex, 1972).

14. Quoted by R.B.J. Walker, op. cit. n. 2 at p. ix.

15. See, J. Ruggie, 'Continuity and Transformation in the World Polity: Toward a Neo-Realist Synthesis', 36 *World Politics* (1983), p. 261; O. Weaver, 'Territory, Authority and Identity: the Late Twentieth-Century Emergence of Neo-Medieval Political Structures in Europe', cited in O. Weaver, 'Identity, Integration, Security' *Journal of International Affairs* (1996), p. 389.

16. It is of course true that in medieval times the Pope and the Holy Roman Emperor had pretensions of exercising supreme and universal political authority. But political identity in those days was religious doctrine, overlaid with assumptions about the universal nature of human community. See further, D. Philpott, 'Sovereignty: An Introduction and Brief History', 48 *Journal of International Affairs*

origins and content of *national* political identity, especially in the territorial state system as it emerged after the Treaty of Westphalia (section 2). Political integration is about identity, loyalty, citizenship and democratic participation but these have remained with the nation-state and have not been projected beyond that level. It is thus vital to understand what exactly the 'shared understandings' in this respect actually consist of. Moreover, understanding the 'historicity'[17] of phenomena assists in the process of mobilising them beyond the status of unquestioned assumptions. Particular attention will be paid to the link between national political identity (citizenship, representative democracy, civil society) as it was consolidated over the centuries and liberal political philosophy (section 3). This is relevant in the present context primarily with regard to the manner in which the principle of democracy was given content in the nation-state as opposed to its original conception and practice by the Ancient Greeks.

Section 4 then turns specifically to the evolution of international organisations as such and briefly looks at the principle of democracy from this perspective of accentuated international cooperation. The conclusion is that the classic intergovernmental organisations did not substantially undermine the principle of democracy as it operated on the national level. This was despite the fact that most of them had no representative organ or parliamentary assembly; the crux was that national parliaments were not sidestepped completely by the national governments in the context of such international organisations. Moreover they did not create a separate legal order with legislative instruments requiring direct application in the national legal system without further national (parliamentary) discretion. Section 5 turns to the specific case of the European Union and attempts to describe why it is that what is referred to as the public realm of politics is systematically undermined as a result of ongoing European integration. This has concretised in the form of a number of so-called 'deficits' which exist at the level of the EU; the problem is that these deficits are not benign ones, which may ultimately as the EU evolves be 'remedied'. They are deficits capable of preventing the organic growth of the system as a whole.

This paper attempts in the final analysis to relate the notion of 'postnational democracy' in the context of the future evolution of the

---

(1995), p. 353. See also, J. van Kan, 'Règles Générales du Droit de la Paix. L'Idée de l'Organisation Internationales dans ses Grandes Phases', *Receuil des Cours de l'Académie de Droit International*, 1938-IV, p. 446 et seq.

17.   The term is that of M. Foucault, quoted by G. Soulier, 'Union Européenne et Dépérissement de l'Etat' in G. Duprat, (ed.) *L'Union Européenne. Droit, Politique, Democratie.* (Paris, 1996), p. 289.

European Union to the (partial) redress of the 'deficit' scenario. The suggestion made that current times are not necessarily as unpropitious for qualitatively different solutions as perursal of daily newspapers might lead us to believe. Two factors in particular stand out in that context: first, the growth 'from below' of a nascent European level 'civil society' and second, the potential offered by advanced information technology in terms of 'imagining' community beyond the level of the nation-state (section 6). Finally, some concluding remarks are made (section 7).

PART I: THE NEWTONIAN FRAME OF REFERENCE OF THE NATION-STATE

2. The Process of Consolidation of National Political Identity

2.1 Politics in the Middle Ages

Stepping back in time then in order to re-examine the transformation which gave rise to the notion of the territorial state as the modern mode of organising political space. This exercise is necessary in order to understand the 'shared understandings' which the notion of the territorial state has itself spawned in the intervening centuries. In particular what role has the principle of state sovereignty played in determing the location of political community? What happens outside the domain of politics (international relations)? Moreover, is there a necessary and inevitable link between the principle of state sovereignty as it was originally conceived and notions of democracy? And what is the relationship between political identity and national culture?

A brief trawl through history will reveal that the question of the location of political community has known a number of transformations.[18] First, the city-state of the Greeks and Romans, with the conceptions of active citizenship and civic virtue and direct democracy by such virtuous citizens.[19] In the small compass of the city-

---

18.   See too, R. Dahl, 'A Democratic Dilemma: System Effectiveness Versus Citizen Participation', 109 *Political Science Quarterly* (1994), p. 23.

19.   See further, M.I. Finley, *Politics in the Ancient World* (Cambridge, 1983). On the revival in Renaissance Italy, see J.G.A. Pocock, *The Machiavellian Moment: Florentine Political Thought and the Atlantic Republican Tradition* (Princeton, 1975).

state, the central institution was the assembly in which all citizens were entitled to participate.[20] But by medieval times a different situation prevailed in the sense that the Pope and the Holy Roman Emperor had pretentions of exercising supreme and universal political authority over a highly fragmentary medieval world.[21] Medieval Europe was in a sense the archetype of non exclusive territorial rule, with its 'patchwork of overlapping and incomplete rights of government' which were 'inextricably superimposed and tangled'.[22] This system of rule had of course a *fragmenting effect* on political organisation. This medieval world was characterised by a hierarchial conception of the relationship between the existing political entities on the one hand and the Emperor on the other. Probably the greatest difference and contrast between the Middle Ages and the modern era is that in the Middle Ages, in spite of the fragmentation, turbulence and sparse contacts, there was a strong emphasis on *unity*.[23] The accent in the modern era has by contrast been on separateness and diversity in the form of the consolidation of equal and sovereign territorial states.[24]

Christian political communities (Church, estates of knights and clergy, cities and their leagues etc) considered themselves as living under a common roof of law. Medieval actors viewed themselves as *the local embodiments of a universal community* which was legitimated by a common discourse of law, religion and custom. This discourse was centred on the principle of *heteronomy*, living under someone else's law, as opposed to sovereignty which denotes a condition of giving the law unto oneself. Neither the Pope nor the Holy Roman Emperor was considered sovereign in a modern sense. In medieval times, political identity was synonymous with *religious doctrine*, overlaid with assumptions about the universal nature of human community.[25] The strength of the idea of the unity of mankind created a spiritual climate

---

20. See, R. Dahl, op. cit. n. 18 at p. 25.

21. See further, J. van Kan, op. cit. n. 16.

22. See, J. Ruggie, 'Territoriality and Beyond: Problematising Modernity in International Relations', 47 *International Organisation* (1993) pp. 139, 149. See also, J.R. Strayer and D.C. Munro, *The Middle Ages* (New York, 1959), p. 115.

23. See, E.N. van Kleffens, 'Sovereignty in International Law', R.A.D.I. 82 (1953) 5, p. 18.

24. Ibid.

25. For descriptions of authority in the Middle Ages, see further, D. Philpott, op. cit. n. 16.

directly opposed to the rise and growth of separate and sovereign states. If we look back then to the medieval system we discover that notions of *space* were organised concentrically around *many centres* depending upon current political affiliations, rather than a singular centre with established territorial boundaries. *Time* was thought of in terms of repetition of the past rather than an unfolding of novel events in a cumulative or progressive sequence.[26] The experience of events was not yet associated with a particular 'national' history.

2.2 The rise of the territorial state

The idea of an omnipotent state was thus remote from the *medieval* mind.[27] Machiavelli's use of the word state (*lo stato*) in *The Prince* is the first modern use of the word state but is more related to the medieval idea of 'standing' or 'condition' as in the term *status regni*.[28] The modern legal meaning of the term state[29] in the sense of an independent continuous public power only truly emerged with French sixteenth century thinkers like Du Haillen, Bude and Bodin.[30] The first really conscious and systematic use of the term sovereignty was by the French

---

26. It was known only as cyclical - seasonal, annual, natural (birth, lifetime, death). See further, J. Agnew and S. Corbridge, *Mastering Space. Hegemony, Territory and International Political Economy*. (London, 1995), pp. 84-85.

27. In the words of one notable scholar, W. Ullmann, *Principles of Government and Politics in the Middle Ages* (London, 1975), p. 137. This position is strengthened by the fact that the word 'state' did not exist in political parlance until the 1500's. However some proponents of the medieval state argue that the state pre-existed the consciously formulated idea by several centuries, see, H. Mitteis, *The State in the Middle Ages: A Comparative Constitutional History of Feudal Europe* (Amsterdam, 1975). See also, J. Strayer, *On the Medieval Origins of the Modern State* (Princeton, 1973).

28. See, J.H. Hexter, *The Vision of Politics on the Eve of the Reformation: More Machiavelli and Seyssel* (London, 1973).

29. See, A. Vincent, *Theories of the State* (Oxford, 1987), p. 18, namely as relating to that of a *public power* which acts separately from both ruler and ruled and constitutes the centralised locus of institutionalised power.

30. See, Q. Skinner, *The Foundations of Modern Political Thought*, Vol. 2, pp. 354-5 (Cambridge, 1978) and K. Dyson, *The State Tradition in Western Europe: A Study of an Idea and an Institution* (Oxford, 1980), p. 28.

thinker Jean Bodin[31] in 1574, although some authors claim that sovereignty existed in fact long before it could be described in theory.[32] In his own terms Bodin thought that he was discussing something hitherto uninvestigated. Sovereignty in his thought was *the defining constitutive power of the state*. For Bodin *res publica* and sovereignty were complementary, inseparable notions. The possession of sovereign power was seen as essential for political stability. The crucial element in Bodin's thought is his recognition of the fact that if the political order is to survive, *power* must in fact rest unchallenged with the sovereign. In other words the element of *force* which Machiavelli and his contemporaries had earlier observed as a largely subterranean aspect was now coming to the surface to be recognised as truly the ultimate guarantor of the state's existence.[33] Sovereignty was described by Bodin as a form of exercising public power, namely 'supreme power over citizens and subjects unrestrained by the laws'. Bodin makes a distinction between law and the laws, and while the sovereign is, according to Bodin, above the particular laws of the country he rules over, yet he is subject, as a member of the general community of the human race, to the divine or natural law and to the law of Nations. In the sixteenth century sovereignty was initially thought of as the supreme authority of *a person*, monarch or emperor.[34]

Although Bodin established that sovereignty was indivisible, the Dutch succeeded, in the aftermath of the Union of Utrecht of 1579 and the formal establishment of the United Provinces, in adding significantly to the complexity of the concept.[35] The provinces very consciously delegated certain powers and retained certain powers. The experience of the Dutch revolt showed that the precise location of sovereignty is not always readily defined. The Dutch managed to refine the idea of sovereignty in order to establish a kind of inner sovereignty which not

---

31.   Bodin's theory of sovereignty was fully formulated in his work *The Six Books of a Commonweale* (1576), designed to meet the problems of order as well as to systematically explore the domain of politics. See, J. Bodin, *Six Books of the Commonwealth*, M. Tooley (ed) (Oxford, 1955).

32.   See, J. Strayer, op. cit. n. 27 at p. 9.

33.   J.H. Shennan, *The Origins of the Modern European State 1450-1725* (London, 1974), p. 74.

34.   For a discussion of the notion of absolute sovereignty and theorists such as Bodin and Hobbes, see A. Vincent, *Theories of the State*, (Oxford, 1987), pp. 45-75.

35.   See, J.H. Shennan, op. cit. n. 33 at p. 84. On the Union of Utrecht in general see, J.C. Boogman, 'The Union of Utrecht: its Genesis and Consequences' in *Van Spel tot Spelers* (The Hague, 1982) pp. 48-82.

even Bodin himself had fully comprehended.[36] Bodin had accepted that sovereignty was in close alliance with force, at the root of all political organisation. The Dutch revolt suggested that force might also push sovereignty into a hitherto unsuspected inner core, like a Russion *matryoshka* doll, one replica within another.[37] This nuclear concept depended in particular upon the force of wealth and commerce,[38] notably that of the province of Holland.

2.3 The consolidation of external and internal sovereignty

The key development in this social time frame in Europe was unquestionably the *Peace of Westphalia of 1648.* This has been described as the 'majestic portal' which led from the old medieval world to a completely new world.[39] What Westphalia did was to give princes *the power to make alliances* - allowing them freedom of action outside their borders. It made the sovereign state the legitimate political unit and implied that basic attributes of statehood such as the existence of a government with *control* of its territory were the criteria for becoming a state.[40] This post-medieval epoch was characterised by the coexistence of a multiplicity of states each sovereign within its territory, equal to one another and free from any external earthly authority. The new multistate system rested on international law and the balance of power, a law operating *between* rather than above states and a power operating *between* rather than above states. This balance of power (*iustum potentiae*

---

36. See further on the Dutch situation, L. Besselink, 'An Open Constitution and European Integration: The Kingdom of the Netherlands', SEW 6 (1996), pp. 192, 194 and P. Verloren van Themaat, 'Einige Betrachtungen über die Zukunft der Europäischen Union aus der Sicht eines weltoffenen Nachbarlandes' in O. Due et al. (eds) *Festschrift Ulrich Everling*, Vol. II, (Baden-Baden, 1995) pp. 1543, 1545-1549.

37. See, J.H. Shennan, op. cit. n. 33 at p. 85.

38. See, J.H. Shennan, op. cit. n. 33 at p. 84.

39. See, L. Gross, 'The Peace of Westphalia, 1648-1948' in L. Gross (ed.) *International Law in the Twentieth Century* (New York, 1969), p. 33.

40. The argument is not that the Peace of Westphalia created a system of sovereign states *ex nihilo* but rather that it consolidated 300 years of evolution toward such a system. See, D. Philpott, op. cit. at n. 16. An even more for-reaching argument claiming that Westphalia was not a decisive break between the medieval and modern worlds can be found in S. Krasner, 'Westphalia and all that' in J. Goldstein and R. Keohane, (eds) *Ideas and Foreign Policy: Beliefs, Institutions and Political Change* (Ithaca, 1993) pp. 235-64.

aequilibrum) was expressly referred to in the Peace Treaty of Utrecht (1713). The inclusive bases of legitimation that had prevailed in the medieval world, articulated in divine and natural law, yielded to the doctrine of sovereignty.[41]

The principle of state sovereignty did not appear out of thin air. It embodies a historically specific account of ethical possibility in the form of an answer to questions about the nature and location of political community.[42] It drew a clear demarcation between life inside and life outside a centred political community. It became clear that sovereignty had *two* faces. The positive 'inside' face of sovereignty referred to a state's power to regulate its own affairs. It entailed full legislative, executive and judicial power and by its nature such inner sovereignty is divisible -among such powers.[43] The principle of (internal) state sovereignty offered a resolution to questions about what political community can be, given the priority of citizenship and particularity over all universalist claims to a common human identity. The negative 'outside' view of sovereignty concerned foreign relations. It prescribed that no sovereign state was subject to the power or control of any external actor. This is what is often referred to as *external sovereignty* and is premised on the unitary nature of the state which was not considered at any stage as capable of being divided up.[44] The outside is the place where political community is impossible. What goes on *between* states is thus in principle quite different from what goes on *within* states:[45] it is *relations* as opposed to politics.

The study of external sovereignty is the concern of international law while the study of the other, internal sovereignty, is the object of constitutional and administrative law.[46] For realist international relations theorists of the day, the pursuit of politics in the classic sense of the pursuit of justice and virtue was not possible in the state's external relations with one another. Only the participants in a territorially bounded state could pursue 'authentic politics'.[47] Instead what happened in the

---

41. See, J. Ruggie, op.cit n. 4 at p. 151.

42. See, R.B.J. Walker, op. cit. n. 2 at p. 62.

43. See, P. Hay, *Federalism and Supranational Organisation*, (Illinois, 1966), p. 64.

44. See, P. Hay, ibid. at p. 70.

45. See, R.B.J. Walker, op. cit. n. 2 at p. 63.

46. See, E.N. van Kleffens, op. cit. n. 23 at p. 29.

47. See, R.B.J. Walker, op. cit. n. 2.

context of international relations was that 'the sovereign states followed their ordered paths in a harmony of mutual attraction and repulsion like the gravitational law that swings planets in their orbits'.[48] The gravitational law was the principle of external sovereignty and the shared understanding that only the participants in a territorially bounded state could pursue 'authentic politics' (internal sovereignty). This statist account of political community was given such a sharp delineation in early modern Europe that it determined ultimately our understanding that the state was the only possible locus of democracy as a system of governance once it emerged in a widespread fashion post the French Revolution.

The French actions from 1789 to 1815 forwarded the general European transition from indirect rule via intermediaries (priests, nobles etc) to *direct rule*.[49] Europe as a whole shifted massively toward *centralised direct rule* with some representation for the ruled.[50] As centralised direct rule expanded throughout Europe, the welfare, culture and daily routines of ordinary Europeans came to depend as never before on which state they happened to reside in.[51] Internally states undertook to impose national languages, national educational systems, national military service and more. Externally they began to control movement across frontiers, to use tarrifs and customs as instruments of economic policy and to treat foreigners as distinctive kinds of people deserving limited rights and close surveillance. Life thus homogenised within states (distinctive characteristics) and heterogenised among states (differentiation).

The discourse of sovereignty also took place internally, relating to the nature of power and rule. Absolutism helped set in motion a process of state-making which began to reduce the social, economic and cultural variation *within states* and expand the variation among them.[52] Sovereignty shifted from the person of the monarch, identified with a 'divine cosmos' to the territory of the state and state institutions (a more impersonal structure of power with supreme jurisdiction over a territory)

---

48.   M. Wight, 'The Balance of Power and International Order' in A. James, (ed.) *The Bases of International Order* (London, 1973), p. 98.

49.   See, C. Tilly, *Coercion, Capital and European States*. AD 990-1992. (Oxford, 1990), at p. 110.

50.   See, C. Tilly, ibid.

51.   See, C. Tilly, ibid. at p. 115.

52.   See, C. Tilly, ibid. at p. 19.

and the loyalty of citizens became something that had to be won by modern states (legitimacy). The idea of state sovereignty was the source of the idea of *impersonal state power*. But it was also the legitimating framework of a centralised power system in which all social groups in the long run wanted a stake.[53] The movement beyond the theory of the personalised absolute sovereign to the idea of the impersonal, abstract state, which controls a consolidated territory and possesses a system of offices that is differentiated from other organisations operating in the same territory was neither identical nor simultanous in different countries.[54]

2.4 'Imagining' and consolidating 'national' identity

At the same time as the emergence of the multi state system as we know it today, the later stages of European state formation produced the phenomenon of *national (political) identification* with the state.[55] National consciousness in this sense consists of an overriding identification of the individual with a culture that is protected by the state.[56] Nationalism has been defined as the striving to make culture and polity congruent.[57] Benedict Anderson has provided a powerful account of how it was only in the modern era that people from diverse locales were able to 'imagine' themselves part of a single community.[58] In Anderson's view the spread of print media through the capitalist market made possible a unity without the mediation of ruling elites made up of literati (the clerisy in Gellner's terminology). It shaped a common sphere of communication exchange in Latin leading to imagined communities of readers with access to the same newspapers, books and journals. Print capitalism thus permitted the unprecedented ability to imagine the simultanous existence of ones co-nationals. *Culture* became national and thus politicised.

Both Anderson and Gellner regard national identity as a distinctive mode of consciousness: the nation as a whole imagining itself to be a

---

53.   See, D. Held, *Democracy and the Global Order* (Oxford, 1995), at p. 46.

54.   See further, K. Dyson, op. cit. n. 30 at p. 29; A. Vincent, op. cit. n. 29 at p. 35.

55.   See, C. Tilly, op. cit. n. 49 at p. 116.

56.   See, in general E. Gellner, *Nations and Nationalism* (Oxford, 1983).

57.   See, E. Gellner, ibid. at p. 43.

58.   B. Anderson, *Imagined Communities* (London, 1991).

unified subject of history.[59] Only within the homogenous territorial space of the modern state could the self-conscious subject of modern history emerge (the nation).

For Rousseau the citizens of a state had put themselves freely but unconditionally 'under the supreme direction of the general will'. The state was considered to be founded upon a *contract* among citizens through which they entrust such powers to a government as is deemed necessary for common protection.[60] This doctrine of popular sovereignty found expression in the US Declaration of Independence in 1776. But it underwent yet another shift with the French revolutionary constitution of 1791 where it assumed the guise of *national sovereignty*. The governing people became a transformed political subject, namely a people of *citizens* which came to be identified with the *Nation*.[61] What the French revolution did was to politicise the cultural concept of nationality.[62] Citizenship became defined by nationality as well as by legal, political and social rights, thereby giving an individual a political identity in terms of the nation.

The main point is that political identity became nationalised in modern Europe to the point where nationality equalled identity (including democratic political identity) became another sort of social fact or social construction that is taken for granted, a cognitive frame in which to threaten nationality is to threaten identity. It is a common knowledge that is both politically defended and socio-psycho-logically embedded in a way that is most difficult to displace. In fact the identification of citizenship with residence in a particular territorial space became the central fact of *political identity*.

---

59. See, in general, E. Bakke, *Towards a European identity?* Arena Working Paper no. 10/1995, Oslo.

60. Rousseau conceived this to exclude any form of representative government since the sovereignty of the people cannot be represented. The only free government is therefore a direct democracy in which the citizens can actually be present at town hall meetings. See further, R.D. Masters, *The Political Philosophy of Rousseau* (Princeton, 1968).

61. See, R. Kearney, op. cit. n. 11 at p. 18.

62. See, D. Heater, *Citizenship: The Civic Ideal in World History, Politics and Education* (London, 1990) at p. 57.

3. Liberal Political Philosophy and the Nation-State

3.1 Liberal citizenship

The tale of the emergence and consolidation of national political identity is closely interwoven with notions of citizenship and of democracy as they developed in the context of the nation-state. Throughout the formative phase of the modern state, the struggle for *membership* in the national political community has largely been synonymous with the attempt to establish a form of popular sovereignty through the entrenchment of civil and political rights.[63] These were the so-called first generation of citizenship rights in T. H. Marshall's classic typology.[64] By civil rights is meant those rights which are necessary for the establishment of individual autonomy, including liberty of the person, freedom of speech, thought and faith, the right to own property and enter into contracts and the right to be treated equally with others before the law. The 18th century was the main developmental phase for civil rights when the rights of the liberty of the individual and full and equal justice before the law became established.[65] Civil rights created new freedoms, freedoms which in the first instance gradually allowed the male citizen liberty from subservience to the place in which he was born and release from the restrictions on occupation created typically by custom or statute.[66]

The establishment of civil rights in the eighteenth century was a significant step in the development of political rights, namely those elements of rights which create the possibility of *participation* in the

---

63. Medieval constitutionalism was based on the idea of *particular liberties*, both for institutions and their participants, on rights linked to status and privilege. Cities, guilds and religious corporations enjoyed privileges, specific and differential grants of power. See further, A. Black, *Guilds and Civil Society in European Political Thought from the Twelfth Century to the Present* (London, 1984). Modern liberalism sought to sweep such privileges away, to destroy status differences and to replace them with equal individual rights. See further, T.H. Marshall, *Citizenship and Social Class* (London, 1973). See also D. Held, *Democracy and the Global Order. From the Modern State to Cosmopolitan Governance.* (Cambridge, 1995), p. 67 and D. Heater, ibid.

64. *Citizenship and Social Class* (London, 1973).

65. See, T.H. Marshall, ibid.

66. See, D. Held, op. cit. n. 63 at p. 67.

exercise of political power as a member of a political association. Even if political rights emerged in the late 18th in some countries, their entrenchment belongs above all to the 19th and 20th centuries.[67] Entrenchment during this period reflects a growing appreciation of the tension between the formal recognition of a person as 'free and equal' in civil matters and the actual liberty of that persons to pursue interests free of political impediment.[68] Political rights were gradually realised as an indispensable part of guaranteeing individual freedom. The establishment of political liberty involved a process whereby the political rights which had previously been the monopoly of the privileged few were extended to the adult population as a whole. Citizenship thus came to be equated with full membership of political society. Later the struggle was one for a second generation of citizenship rights, namely 'social' citizenship (social and economic rights, welfare etc).[69] Environmental rights belong to the 'third generation' of rights, having come onto the political agenda as a result of the increasing pollution of the environment in the late twentieth century.[70]

The political philosophy which informed the foundational development of citizenship was the political philosophy of liberalism.[71] Liberalism in this sense describes a tradition of thought that emphasises tolerance and respect for individual rights and that runs (among others) from John Locke, Immanuel Kant and John Stuart Mill to John Rawls.[72] The result of this historical contingence was that citizenship in its modern form crystallised in many Western polities in the form of civil and political rights above all else. The emphasis was thus on individual freedom and autonomy and not on participation, civic virtue or active citizenship in the classical Athenian tradition of a 'total citizen'.[73] The Greeks did not entertain a positive notion of the individual as a person,

---

67.   See further, T.H. Marshall. op. cit. n. 64.

68.   See, D. Held, op. cit. n. 63 at p. 68.

69.   These are beyond the subject of this paper. See further, T.H. Marshall, op. cit. n. 64.

70.   See further, D. Oliver and D. Heater, *The Foundations of Citizenship* (1994), p. 92 et seq.

71.   See further, M.J. Sandel, *Liberalism and the Limits of Justice* (Cambridge, 1982).

72.   See, M.J. Sandel, *Democracy's Discontent. America in Search of a Public Philosophy.* (Harvard, 1996), p. 4.

73.   See further, N.D. Fustel de Coulanges, *La Cité Antique* (Paris, 1878), p. 396.

with a legitimate *private space* or personal rights.[74] Jellinek well summarised the point:

'In ancient times man was never definitely recognised as a person ... Only the nineteenth century has scored a general victory with the principle: "man is a person"'.[75]

Real self-government as the Greeks practised it required the citizen to devote himself completely to the public service. Governing one self meant spending one's life governing -it produced a political animal at the expense of *homo oeconomicus*. Aristotle remarked that a man who has to work in order to live cannot be a citizen.[76] The Athenian city-state shared features with republican Rome. Both sought to foster a deep sense of public duty, a tradition of 'civic virtue'. Classical republicanism received its most robust restatement in the early Renaissance, especially in the city-states of Italy.[77] The republican conception of freedom, unlike the liberal conception, requires a formative politics, cultivating in citizens the qualities of character which (direct) self-government requires.[78]

Modern liberal democracy on the other hand is meant to protect the freedom of the individual as a person - a freedom that cannot be entrusted, as Benjamin Constant said, to the 'subjection of the individual to the power of the whole'.[79]

3.2 Liberal Democracy

The etymological definition of democracy stems from the combination of two Greek words: *demos* (people) and *kratos* (power), literally power of

---

74.   See, G. Sartori, *The Theory of Democracy Revisited* (New Jersey, 1987), p. 285.

75.   Quoted by G. Sartori, ibid. at p. 285.

76.   Quoted by G. Sartori, ibid. at p. 282.

77.   See further, J.G.A. Pocock, *The Machiavellian Moment: Florentine Political Thought and the Atlantic Republican Tradition* (Princeton, 1975).

78.   See, M. Sandel, *Democracy's Discontent. America in Search of a Public Philiosophy* (Harvard, 1996), p. 6. See too, R. Dahl, *Democracy and its critics* (New Haven, 1989), pp. 24-28.

79.   B. Constant, 'The liberty of the Ancients compared to that of the Moderns' in B. Fontana (ed.), *Benjamin Constant Political Writings* (Cambridge, 1988).

the people.[80] When the formula of popular sovereignty is completed it reads thus: democracy is the power of the people over the people.[81] Ancient democracy was conceived in intrinsic symbiotic relation with the *polis*: *politeia* in fact meant both citizenship and the structure (the form) of the *polis*. It was *horizontal* in nature, relying on the active participation of the citizens themselves in the direct *exercise* of power. The democracy of the Ancients qualified as *an observable direct democracy* for it resolved itself not only in the gathering of the citizens in a single place but in an observable behaviour of the participants.[82] The magnitude of the *polis* that allows for such observability is in the order of several thousands: Aristotle spoke in terms of a maximum of 5000.[83]

When the idea of self-government was broached in the context of the newly emerged territorial state it was defined by two features. First the size or scale determined that participation in the *polis*, the territorial state, could not be directly in the *exercise of power* as such. Second the contemporary liberal emphasis on individual freedom and personal rights meant that democratic participation was viewed through this prism. Democracy thus entered the modern world by becoming liberalised.[84] The liberal state came first and thus the ends and values of democracy were translated into the shape of liberal democratic values. In the words of an eminent scholar:

'Democracy *tout court* is far older than liberalism. It is only if we speak of *liberal democracy* that we are speaking of a democracy that comes after liberalism and that is younger than liberalism'.[85]

---

80.   See further, G. Sartori, op. cit. n. 74, p. 21 et seq. In the Greek democracies the *demos* excluded not only women but also slaves.

81.   See, G. Sartori, op. cit. n. 74, p. 30. Or as Lincoln put it in his Gettysburg address of 1863: government of the people, by the people, for the people. See further, A. Barnett, 'The creation of democracy' in P. Hirst and S. Khilnani, *Reinventing Democracy* (Oxford, 1996), pp. 157, 160 and critically, G. Sartori, op. cit. n. 74 at p. 34 who maintains that Lincoln's formula does not suffice to define democracy -its democratic credentials stem rather from Lincoln himself.

82.   See, G. Sartori, op. cit. n. 74 at p. 111.

83.   See, G. Sartori, op. cit. n. 74 at p. 278.

84.   See, B. Barber, *Strong Democracy. Participatory Politics for a New Age* (Berkeley, 1984).

85.   G. Sartori, op. cit. n. 74 at p. 382. His view was that in substance liberalism has prevailed over democracy 'in the sense that it has absorbed democracy far more than democracy has annexed liberalism' (p. 373).

Democracy and (political) liberalism joined forces as and from the revolution of 1848. This link had already been made by de Tocqueville[86] in terms of *equality in freedom*.[87] Political liberalism in this sense stood for the rule of law and the constitutional state; liberty was political freedom expounded by political theorists such as Locke, Blackstone, Montesquieu, Madison and Constant. Political freedom in the liberal democratic mode was defined largely as a negative freedom *for* the citizen *from* state oppression.[88] The constitutional state was born as a minimal state, set up to uphold a liberty from government and which expressed a basic distrust of power.[89]

Representative democracy was an *indirect* form of democracy premised on the notion of delegation of power by the people to representatives. It was individual in the sense that personal or individual freedom was the requisite constituent element.[90] Such *vertical democracy* inevitably entailed that the people as such could only expect to limit and control power as exercised by others but not to exercise it directly themselves. The techniques of vertical representative democracy are election procedures, the representational transmission of power and limited majority rule,[91] all premised on the freedom of the individual to vote (express dissent) and stand for election.

The *demos* (the people) only actually govern at elections, between elections the people's power is largely quiescent; there is also a wide margin of discretion between broad electoral choices and concrete governmental decisions.[92] Various theories exist to describe how representative democracies work and perform - Schumpeter's competitive theory of democracy,[93] Dahl's polyarchy,[94] Bachrach's theory of

---

86. A. de Tocqueville, *Democracy in America* (original edition, 1837).

87. Not freedom in equality: see, A. Barnett, op. cit. n. 81 at p. 165 and G. Sartori, op. cit. n. 74 at p. 373.

88. See, G. Sartori, op. cit. at p. 380.

89. See, G. Sartori, op. cit. at pp. 380-1.

90. See, G. Sartori, op. cit. at p. 368.

91. G. Sartori, op. cit. at p. 30 and *passim*.

92. See, G. Sartori, op. cit. at p. 86.

93. *Capitalism, Socialism and Democracy* (London, 1943), p. 269.

94. *A preface to democratic theory* (Chicago, 1956).

democratic (anti-)elitism,[95] to mention but a few. It is beyond the scope of this paper to discuss these elaborate theories.[96] I would however mention the American political scientist, Benjamin Barber, who coined the term 'thin democracy' for representative (vertical) democracy which makes accountability its primary virtue.[97] Thin (representative) democracy, it is claimed, destroys participation and has a weak view of citizenship.[98]

What I do want to briefly introduce at this point is a type of decision-making commonly found in many advanced liberal democracies, *pluralism*. Pluralist decision-making refers to a mode of discussion in which private interests bargain with each other over how to maximise their own interests.[99] From this perspective the competitive economic market where citizens may express their individual desires on a level playing field contitutes the ideal. Philosophically the core of the pluralist thought is the belief that there is no such thing as common good or 'public interest', just private interests in aggregate forming an overall social utility.[100] A variation is the corporatist tradition of decision-making which recognises the importance of the many intermediate associations in society but assigns a dominant role to particular groups

---

95.   *The Theory of Democratic Elitism: a Critique* (Boston, 1967).

96.   But see, G. Sartori, op. cit. n. 74 at pp. 131-181 and R. Dahl, *Democracy and its Critics* (New Haven, 1989).

97.   See, *Strong Democracy*, op. cit. n. 84.

98.   See, B. Barber, ibid. at pp. 221-3.

99.   See further the detailed analysis contained in C.R. Sunstein, 'Interest Groups in American Public Law', 38 *Stanford Law Review* (1985), p. 29. See also, in particular on the differences of opinion within pluralism, P.P. Craig, *Public law and democracy in the United Kingdom and the United States of America* (Oxford, 1990).

100. For a defence of pluralism see R. Dahl, *Dilemmas of Pluralist Democracy: Autonomy versus Control* (New Haven, 1982). See too, F. Vibert, who in effect seeks to apply a version of pluralism to the European Union, namely what he terms a 'prudential' approach, in: *Europe: A Constitution for the Millennium* (Aldershot, 1995). For a virulent critique of the pluralist model as it operates in the United States in particular see, J-M. Guehenno, *La Fin de la Démocratie* (Paris, 1993).

which represent and articulate the demands of other interest groups in the same sphere.[101]

Electoral power may be the mechanical guarantee of liberal democracy but the substantive guarantee is given by the conditions under which the citizen gets the *information* about the manner in which decision-making takes place and is exposed to the pressure of opinion makers. If this is taken seriously then elections are the means to an end, the end being a 'government of opinion' that is a government responsive to and responsible towards public opinion. Ultimately, 'the opinion of the governed is the real foundation of all government'.[102] As Thomas Jefferson put it almost two hundred years ago:

> 'I know of no safe depository of the ultimate power of the society but the people themselves, and if we think them not enlightened enough to exercise their control with a wholesome discretion, the remedy is not to take it from them, but *to inform their discretion*.'[103]

Even within the representative democracy model, the genesis of the will and opinion of the *demos* that elections limit themselves to recording can be regarded as the real foundation of government. That is why the whole issue of freedom of information is so critical to a proper understanding of liberal democracy. Democratic government functions by definition through widespread *public deliberations* on important issues. Democracy demands transparence, that the house of power be a house of glass

---

101. Such intermediate groups can operate at the expense of those excluded and it is often difficult to assess the claims of such groups to be representative. See further, P.C. Schmitter and G. Lehmbruch (eds.), *Trends Towards Corporatist Intermediation* (London, 1979) and M.L. Harrison, (ed.), *Corporatism and the Welfare State* (Aldershot, 1984). See too, D. Obradovic for consideration of this issue in relation to the European Union, 'Prospects for Corporatist Decision-Making in the EU: The Social Policy Agreement', 2 *Journal of European Public Policy* (1995), p. 261. More recently certain authors have developed the theory of so-called 'associative democracy' namely the transfer of certain functions of government to voluntary organisations on the grounds that they are closer to the people and will carry out these tasks more efficiently. The broad range of (social and economic) self governing institutions are conceived in order to restore the ideal of a committed public service in the face of widespread bureaucratic failure. See further, P. Hirst, *Associative Democracy* (Cambridge, 1994) and J. Cohen and J. Rogers (eds.) *Associations and Democracy* (London, 1995).

102. See, A.V. Dicey, *Lectures on the Relation between Law and Public Opinion in England during the Nineteenth Century* (London, 1905), p. 3.

103. Quoted by B. Barber, op. cit. n. 84.

(according to the literal meaning of the word). Secrecy can be said to lie at the very core of power.[104] Democracy cannot exist without an informed and thus enlightened people. How can citizens be expected to obey laws when they have not been privy to the reasons for their adoption? Let alone have confidence in the administration in question. But rather than letting the sun shine through clear panes of glass, power has a tendency to settle comfortably behind opaque constructions, facilitating the appearance of mystery and unclear structures of responsibility.

Transparency is crucial to a proper understanding of liberal democracy as it has developed, I would therefore like to devote it some further attention. Under liberal democratic systems legislation is adopted by Parliament. The general rule prevailing in the liberal democratic systems of Western Europe and further afield is that legislative assemblies operate under the full glare of publicity whenever they are carrying out their legislative function. This is regarded as an absolutely essential component of the liberal democratic systems prevailing in those countries. Information is the currency of democracy. This means that open sessions of plenary sittings of legislative organs take place, in the majority of cases open (parliamentary) committee sessions where legislation is under consideration (as opposed to matters mandating more confidential treatment such as internal security or monetary policy etc.), all draft legislation is published as are *verbatim* reports of debates etc.[105] Legislators thus conduct their debates in public with arguments and counter arguments recorded in published minutes. The process of public deliberation is further facilitated by the accountability of government ministers to parliament, the supervision of such external bodies as the court of auditors and the law courts, and by enabling members of the public to request access to official documents. The belief underpinning such 'publicity' is that the quality of the ultimate decisions will be improved not only by the public's contribution to the decision-making process itself but perhaps even more by the knowledge of the decision makers that they are acting in the public view. General understanding and acceptance of their purpose may thereby be increased.

The concept of a unified civil service or administration to implement the policy decisions of elected politicians is one of the traditional tenets of a liberal democracy. Since Max Weber observed the characterising features of administrative organisation and labelled them

---

104. See, E. Canetti, *Crowds and Power* (London, 1960), p. 338.

105. See further, D. Curtin and H. Meijers, 'The Principle of Open Government in Schengen and the European Union: Democratic Retrogression?', 32 CML Rev. (1995) p. 391.

'bureaucracy' some kind of unified administration has formed a recognised part of the state in most liberal democracies.[106] As a result of the substantial increase in the powers of bureacracies in modern times, parliamentary control has become less effective in practice.[107] One attempt in modern times to make bureacracy unthreatening is its subjection to the rule of law, in particular in the process of empowering the courts to review and if necessary to overturn the actions of bureacracies.[108]

The technical nature of issues to be resolved often place professionals in a better position than individual citizens.[109] Expert decision-making processes are sometimes described by the term *synoptic* decision-making, namely the exchange of data by professionals so that they can then apply preset scientific rules to determine the optimal decision.[110] One palpable result of increasing reliance on expert decision-making is that the expansion of the knowledge gap[111] between professionals, specialists, experts and the majority of ordinary people has increased very dramatically. During the course of the 1960's in particular, there was a noticeable and growing belief in many liberal democratic countries that a more open approach to the operation of government would increase the possibility of improving the control over the workings of the administration of government (the executive power) as well as stimulating an informed debate on government policy. The measures adopted in many liberal democratic countries included mechanisms to increase the public participation in the administrative decision-making process as well as to reinforce provisions dealing with improved explanation and justification of decisions to the public. In addition a substantial number of the countries which now belong to the European Union also adopted the principle whereby information held by

---

106. See, M. Weber, *Economy and Society*, op. cit. n. 5 at pp. 956-1005.

107. See further, Y. Meny, 'L'evolution des fonctions des parlements' *Les regimes politiques européenes en perspective*, Cahiers Français No. 268, p. 44.

108. See further, L. Jaffe, *Judicial control of administrative action* (Boston, 1965).

109. See, in particular, G.E. Frug, 'The Ideology of Bureacracy in America', 97 *Harvard Law Review* (1984), p. 1277. See too at the international level the rise of 'epistemic communities' P.M. Haas, 'Introduction: Epistemic Communities and International Policy Coordination', 46 *International Organisation* (1992), p. 1.

110. See, C.S. Diver, 'Policymaking paradigms in administrative law', 95 Harv. L. Rev. (1981), p. 393.

111. See, G. Sartori, op. cit. n. 74 at p. 432.

public authorities is generally open to the public unless such access has been explicitly exempted for a limited number of specified reasons.[112]

3.3 The role of civil society

A democratic state is widely held to be inconceivable without a democratic *society*. Central to classical liberalism (as earlier defined) is the distinction between the public and the private spheres.[113] The public sphere is based on representative government and the rule of law (the constitutional state). Its purpose is both to govern and to protect the private sphere (private property and individual rights). The state is the public and political sphere, limited in its scope and functions. The private sphere is that of individual action, contract and market exchange, protected by and yet independent of the state.[114]

Since its inception liberal political theory has regarded its main objective as the preservation of an extensive sphere of action independent of the state and has seen this as an essential complement to and support of the formal political institutions of representative government.[115] Civil society is defined as a sphere of social interaction between the economy and state, composed above all of the intimate sphere (especially the family), the sphere of associations (especially voluntary associations), social movements and forms of public communication.[116] The conception is of civil society as a spontaneous order independent of and separate from the state and thus in a sense prior to politics and non

---

112. At one end of the spectrum is *Sweden* with a long and well established tradition of openness of the administrative arm of governance. Other Member States applied the principle of open government to the administration only much more recently but nonetheless consider its status as fundamental. An example from this category is *the Netherlands*. Others still only allow individuals access to documents where they have a personal interest in them, with a view to judicial proceedings and have no general access to information legislation (*Germany and Ireland*). See for details, Curtin and Meijers, 'Openbaarheid in Europa. Geheim Bestuur door Schengen en Maastricht?', NJB (1995), pp. 158-180.

113. See, P. Hirst, 'Democracy and Civil Society' in P. Hirst and S. Khilnani, *Reinventing Democracy* (Oxford, 1996), pp. 97, 98.

114. See, P. Hirst, ibid.

115. See, P. Hirst, ibid. at p. 98.

116. See, J.L. Cohen and A. Arato, *Civil Society and Political Theory* (Massachusetts, 1995), p. ix.

political.[117] It is created though forms of self-constitution and self mobilisation.[118]

A non-governmental civic (public) space is voluntary and is constituted by freely associated individuals and groups; it aims at common ground and consensual (integrative and collaborative) modes of action. Secondary associations can in theory at any rate function as so-called 'seedbeds of civic virtue': the associations of civil society can foster personal moral development, social connectedness and civic values that support liberalism.[119] Actors in civil society need the protection of an institutionalised legal order to guard their autonomy and freedom of action. Thus civil society not only restricts state power but legitimates state authority when that authority is based on the rule of law.[120]

The powerful imagery of civil society held the key to America's early democratic energy and civic activism. In de Tocqueville's America, society comprised three sectors: government and private but also the third arena of civil society.[121] In that era a modest governmental sphere and an unassuming private sector were overshadowed by an extensive civil society tied together by school, church, town and voluntary association. Citizens and associations together comprised civil society. Only later did civil society as thus defined lose ground. Corporations, legitimised as 'legal persons' and limited liability partnerships, supplanted voluntary associations as the primary actors on the non-governmental side.[122] In current usage the term 'civil society' no longer includes the economy as constituted by private law.[123] Rather its institutional core comprises non-governmental   and   non-economic   connections   and   voluntary

---

117. See, P. Hirst, op. cit. n. 113 at p. 98. See too, B. Barber, op. cit. n. 84 at p. 147.

118. See, J.L. Cohen and A. Arato, op. cit. n. 116 at p. ix.

119. See, N.R. Rosenblum, 'Civil Societies: Liberalism and the Moral Uses of Pluralism', 61 *Social Research* (1994) pp. 539, 544.

120. See, L. Diamond, 'Rethinking Civil Society. Toward Democratic Consolidation' *Journal of Democracy* (1995), p. 4.

121. See further, A. de Tocqueville, *Democracy in America*, (original edition, 1837). For a historical perspective see, A. Black, *Guilds and Civil Society in European Thought from the Twelfth Century to the Present* (London, 1984).

122. See, B. Barber, 'Three Challenges to Reinventing Democracy' in P. Hirst and S. Khilnani, *Reinventing Democracy* (Oxford, 1996), p. 151.

123. See, J. Habermas, *Between Facts and Norms. Contributions to a Discourse Theory of Law and Democracy,* (MIT, 1996), p. 366.

associations that constitute a civic space. The potential is that a rich associational life can supplement the role of political parties in stimulating political participation, increasing the political efficacy and skill of democratic citizens and promoting an appreciation of the obligations as well as the rights of democratic citizenship.[124] 'Freedom of association', de Tocqueville mused, may 'after having agitated society for some time ... strengthen the state in the end'.[125]

Institutionalised opinion and will-formation processes of the demos (see *supra* in the discussion on liberal democracy) depend on supplies coming from the informal contexts of communication found in civil society.[126] Opinion-forming associations which specialise in issues and contributions and are generally designed to generate influence, belong to the civil society infrastructure of a public sphere dominated by the mass media.[127] Jurgen Habermas has termed this the political public sphere, 'a communication structure rooted in the lifeworld through the associational network of civil society'.[128]

PART TWO: THE INTERNATIONAL FRAME OF REFERENCE

4. Intergovernmental Organisations: Diplomacy not Democracy

4.1 Introduction

It has emerged from the above discussion that the Newtonian frame of reference of the nation-state comprised essentially (for my purposes at any rate) four lines of inquiry. First the principle of state sovereignty which underlined the clear demarcation between life inside and life

---

124. See further, C. Offe, 'New Social Movements: Challenging the Boundaries of Institutional Politics', 52 *Social Research* (1985) p. 817; R. Koopmans, 'New Social Movements and Changes in Political Participation in Western Europe', 19 *West European Politics* (1996), p. 28.

125. A. de Tocqueville, op. cit. n. 86, 2:126.

126. See, J. Habermas, *Between Facts and Norms*. op. cit. n. 123 at p. 352.

127. J. Habermas, op. cit. n. 123 at p. 355.

128. Op. cit. n. 123 at p. 359.

outside a centred political community. Life outside the territorial state came to be understood as the place where political community was impossible. Second, the identification of citizenship with residence in a particular territorial state became the central fact of (national) political identity. Third, liberal (nation-state) democracy emphasised the protection of the freedom of the individual as a person and the delegation of power to representatives. Finally, civil society was conceived as largely prior to the state and outside the domain of politics.

The theorists who developed the doctrine of sovereignty were not interested in the relations of states *inter se*; they all thought of the singular state *in abstracto*, and paid comparatively little attention to the question as to how a theory of sovereignty could be applied in a world containing a fair number of states.[129] The international lawyer, on the other hand, is concerned not with the state *in abstracto* but with the *states* whose very *co-existence* is his chief starting point, and he therefore requires a theory which is at least consistent with the relations which he finds exists between them.[130] The relations were ones of coexistence and an unstable balance of power. The realist theory of international relations in the sense of a *realpolitik* view of states[131] quickly became the dominant theory, the leading school of international relations. The great classics of international law have however stressed the relative character of state sovereignty in the face of higher rules as early as Grotius and Vattel. But, as one author put it, there was a joker in the pack: the international law which was to control sovereigns was controlled by them.[132] It tended, understandably enough, primarily to reflect their preoccupation with their own rights and status and dignity.

The Westphalian model of international relations has been characterised by (so-called) classical liberalism, supplemented by realism.[133] As with the nation-state, the dominant theory of international relations was one firmly grounded in liberalism, that is

---

129. See, van Kleffens, op. cit. n. 23 at p. 52.

130. See, van Kleffens, op. cit. n. 23 at p. 53.

131. See further, R.B.J. Walker, op. cit. n. 2.

132. I.L. Claude, *Swords into Plowshares. The Problems and Progress of International Organisation* (Michigan, 1956), p. 19.

133. See further, D. Held, *Democracy and the Global Order* (Oxford, 1995), p. 74 et seq.

liberal political theory transposed onto international society.[134] However where domestic liberal theory appeals to a conception of the individual as a bearer of rights and a democratic actor, international liberalism substitutes the state for the individual and posits the nation-state as the free and equal object and subject of international law.[135] Although autonomous, the state, like the individual, respects the equal rights of his peers.[136]

At the level of the state, liberal political philosophy is premised on the ideal of representativeness as the basis of the state's legitimacy. In international society *consent* replaces representativeness as the prevailing liberal metaphor.[137] Classical liberals are committed to the idea that international law is a creation of the general will of states expressed through their collective consent. In other words the formation of norms can only be through state consent. Any representativeness that there might be is through the state itself. This theory of classical liberalism has been severely deflated by various critiques, including democratic critiques. This has led to the development of a theory of so-called 'democratic liberalism' questioning the democratic credentials of a large number of the states which make up the international order[138] (see further, *infra.* 4.2.1).

In any event, while the concept of the modern state projected the possibility of impartial administration and accountability *within* communities, it did not make the extension of these notions across peoples and nations a central part of the meaning of the conception of political community. Political integration as such (characterised by notions of identity, loyalty, citizenship, and democratic participation)

---

134. See further, A-M. Burley, 'Toward an Age of Liberal Nations', 33 *Harvard International Law Journal* (1992), p. 393 and D. Otto, 'Nongovernmental Organisations in the United Nations System: the Emerging Role of International Civil Society', 18 *Human Rights Quarterly* (1996), p. 107.

135. See further, G.J. Simpson, 'Some Recent Theoretical Orientations in International Law', unpublished paper. The state, like the individual in liberal theory posseses a zone of private action into which the law cannot interfere. The right to privacy of individuals is converted into a states immunity from interference, namely the doctrine of domestic jurisdiction. Similarily the taboo on violence in national law is mirrored by the use of force jurisprudence in international law.

136. See, van Kleffens, op. cit. n. 23 at p. 71.

137. See further, G.J. Simpson, op. cit. n. 135.

138. See, in particular, F.R. Teson, 'The Kantian Theory of International Law', 92 *Columbia Law Review* (1992) p. 53 and T.M. Franck, 'The Emerging Right to Democratic Governance', 86 *American Journal of International Law* (1992), p. 46.

remained exclusively within the nation-state and has not been projected to the international level. The idea of democracy has been very marginal in the context of international relations. Diplomacy not democracy was the operative idea-structure of international relations. Hedley Bull aptly defined diplomatic culture as 'the common stock of ideas and values possessed by the official representatives'.[139] Diplomacy was conducted by the executive branches of national governments, in processes that were only weakly integrated into the internal democratic process. Philip Allott describes the process in colourful language as follows:

'states continued to behave in relation to each other externally in the old familar way, as quasi-persons, more or less as feudal barons, treating their national territory as a power-conferring landholding, the source of what was called their "sovereign power" or "sovereignty". The external theory of society was scarcely more than the pursuit of the so-called national interest by the exercise of power, power that might be exercised in any form dictated by utilitarian and instrumental considerations.'[140]

4.2 The process of international organisation and the principle of democracy

The very process of international organisation as we have known it in Europe since the middle of the 18th century was conceived and implemented so as to respect the primordial role of the territorial state as the sole location of political community. The basic principle of international relations was that the locus of politics remained absolutely *internal* to the participating states and was unaffected even by highly institutionalised international cooperation. International organisation, in the words of Inis Levy Claude, was brought about not so much by prophets who saw it as the legitimate sucessor to sovereign states, as by statesmen who sought new arrangements and devices whereby the sovereign units of the old system could pursue their interests and manage their affairs in the altered circumstances of the age of communication and industrialism.[141] Cooperation not integration was the *leitmotif* of the

---

139. See, H. Bull, *Anarchial Society* (London, 1977), pp. 173-183. See too, H. Nicholson, *Diplomacy* (London, 1963), A. Watson, *Diplomacy: The Dialogue between States* (London, 1982), J. Der Derian, *On Diplomacy* (Oxford, 1987).

140. P. Allott, op. cit. n. 6 at pp. 2490-2491.

141. See, I.L. Claude, op. cit. n. 132 at p. 20.

pre-1945 international organisations.[142] Of course as the 20th century advanced, international organisations grew more sophisticated and more universal in scope, touching on sensitive national interests and there were clear indications that the 'internal sovereignty' of states was indeed affected by the process of international organisation as such.[143] What has been called a 'paradigm shift' in public international law was brought about by the post-1945 'age of integration' in international organisations.[144]

It is well beyond the scope of this paper to document the rise and expansion of intergovernmental organisations.[145] I limit my consideration and focus to the question of how intergovernmental activity in the context of international organisations relates to the principle of democratic decision-making applied in the internal context of the nation-state. In so doing I wish to distinguish briefly two questions. First what might be termed *internal democracy*, namely the extent to which international law and in particular the constituent charters of international organisations were premised on the Member States internally applying (liberal) democratic methods of decision-making. Second, *external democracy*, namely the extent to which the internal decision-making of the intergovernmental organisations itself respected the principle of democratic decision-making.

---

142. See further, E.-U. Petersmann, 'Constitutional Functions of Public International Law' in *Restructuring the International Economic Order: The Role of Law and Lawyers* (Deventer, 1987), p. 49. See too, W. Friedmann, *The Changing Structure of International Law* (London, 1964), p. 60 et seq.

143. In particular in the field of human rights protection a reconceptualised internal sovereignty could be discerned in which a state accepts that violations of human rights will no longer be an issue solely within its internal jurisdiction. For example, the European Convention on Human Rights and the practices of the European human rights system has been described as 'a substantial retreat from the previously sacred principle of national sovereignty': see, P. Sieghart, *The Lawful Rights of Mankind: An Introduction to the International Legal Code of Human Rights* (Oxford, 1985), pp. 67-68. See also, R. Higgins, 'The European Convention on Human Rights' in T. Meron, (ed.), *Human Rights in International Law: Legal and Policy Issues* (Oxford, 1984), p. 538. See, more generally, P. Tangney, 'The New Internationalism: The Cession of Sovereign Competences to Supranational Organisations and Constitutional Change in the United States and Germany' 21 *Yale Journal of International Law* (1996), p. 395.

144. See, E.-U. Petersmann, op. cit. n. 142.

145. See further, H. Schermers and N. Blokker, *International Institutional law* (Dordrecht, 1995).

4.2.1   Internal democracy and international organisations

Internal democracy in the context of international organisations refers basically to the idea that international law can be developed in such a way as to reinforce democratic government within states on the oft-quoted premise that democracies do not wage war with one another.[146] The response of international organisations and international law has been to stress increasingly that international status should depend upon a particular form of domestic governance, namely the liberal democratic method of governance. This has been captured by the phrase 'the right to a democratic governance'[147] or the philosophy of 'democratic liberalism'.[148]

What is however a relatively new development at the international level is an emergent theory of international law which is based on the *dual* consent of states *and individuals*.[149] Those who support a norm of democratic governance ask us to envisage international law as the *law of* as well as between states. The idea is that state consent needs to be supplemented by individual or democratic consent in international law.

In modern international law this idea can be traced back to Woodrow Wilson's idealism at the end of the Great War in 1918. Faced with the devastating results of World War I and the bankruptcy of the Concert of Europe (1818), the *League of Nations* attempted a novel solution, without essentially departing from the Peace of Westphalia. It drew its inspiration from the Concert, the Hague Peace Conferences and the experience of the 19th and 20th centuries in functional international collaboration. The result was the first universal international organisation, the League of Nations, in which the member states assumed certain commitments to cooperate in various fields and above all, without abolishing the right of war, to establish 'the undertakings of international law as the actual rule of *conduct among governments*'.[150]

The League of Nations was a product of its times in the sense of expressing in ideological terms on the international level the philosophy

---

146. This seems to be true: see, E. Weede, 'Some simple calculations on democracy and war involvement' 29 *Journal of Peace Research* (1992), p. 377.

147. See, T. Franck, op. cit. n. 138.

148. See, in particular, F. Teson, op. cit. n. 138.

149. See further, C. Grossman and D. Bradlow, 'Are we being Propelled Towards a People Centered Transnational Legal Order?' 9 *American University Journal of International Law and Policy* (1993), p. 1.

150. See further, I.L. Claude, op. cit. n. 132.

of 19th century liberalism. Following the thesis laid down more than a hundred years earlier by Kant in his essay on *Perpetual Peace* the nascent idea was that world peace could only be established by a compact among democratically governed nations.[151] This vision called for *internal democracy* as a precondition for international cooperation in an institutionalised fora. The assumption was that the age of democracy had arrived, providing a sufficient number of soundly democratic states to unite in an organisation for maintaining world peace. This view has been reinforced in the context of international organisations such as the Council of Europe which, by including newly democratic members from Eastern Euope, has become a pan European body. Moreover the role of the Organisation for Security and Cooperation in Europe (OSCE) in promoting the democratic standards that will enable East and West to come closer together has been significant.

The major international treaties spell out the essentials of democracy, understood as the right of all citizens to participate in the political life of their societies.[152] The idea of democracy reflected in these instruments is not a simple majoritarian one but rather reflects the idea that every person, whether a member of a majority or a minority, has basic rights, including a right to participate in public life.[153] Recently some scholars have sought to argue that democracy (more specifically the right to vote in free and fair elections) has achieved universal recognition as an international legal right.[154] Others carry this emphasis on individuals to its logical conclusion by legitimising intervention in the affairs of a foreign sovereign when necessary to vindicate the rights of its people.[155]

---

151. The self governing qualification for new members specified in article 1 of the Covenant was in practice interpreted to mean only that approximate independence was the standard of eligibility for League membership. See, I.L. Claude, op.cit n. 132 at p. 47.

152. Universal Declaration of Human Rights of 1948, Article 21; International Covenant on Civil and Political Rights, Article 25; European Convention on Human Rights, Article 3 of protocol 1; American Convention on Human Rights, Article 23. See further, T. Franck, op. cit. n. 138 and J. Crawford, 'Democracy in International law', Inaugural Lecture, March 1993, Cambridge University.

153. See, J. Crawford, ibid. at p. 5.

154. See, T. Franck, 'The Emerging Right to Democratic Governance', 86 AJIL (1992), p. 46; T. Meron, 'Democracy and the Rule of Law', 153 *World Affairs* (1990), p. 23; H.J. Steiner, 'Political participation as a Human Right', 1 *Harvard Human Rights YearBook* (1988), p. 77.

155. See, F. Teson, op. cit. n. 138.

But under international law in general (apart from treaties) there was no general endorsement of a principle of democracy.[156] There was no requirement that the government of a state, to be a government, should have been democratically elected or even that it should have the general support of its people. As Oppenheim pointed out in the first edition of his standard text, published in 1905, the actual *control* of a government over the apparatus of the state has been treated as sufficient.[157]

4.2.2   External democracy and international organisations

A vision of political liberalism also called for *external democracy* in the sense of an assumption that the democratic method of arriving at agreement by civilised discussion rather than coercive dictation could be applied to the relations of democratic states as well as individuals. When the League of Nations was founded the thinking was that in the new era which had been launched sovereignty could be a symbol of liberty in international relations. The new era was to be characterised by open diplomacy, the publication of treaties, the investigation and dissemination of facts concerning international disputes, and the use of the League forum to submit grave issues to the moral consciousness of free peoples.[158]

The reality has on the whole not lived up to such grandiose expectations. Certain features of classical international law are intrinsically undemocratic.[159] Of particular relevance is the fact that the executive enjoys more or less comprehensive power in international affairs. Generally the Head of State and the Minister for Foreign Affairs have plenary powers to make international commitments on behalf of the state, and to agree to and apply rules of international law which may affect the rights or claims of individuals without their consent and even

---

156. See, J. Crawford, op. cit. n. 152 at p. 7.

157. L. Oppenheim, *International Law* (London, 1905), Vol. 1, pp. 403 and 405.

158. See further, I.L. Claude, op. cit. n. 132.

159. Such as the fact that the individual has no autonomous procedural remedies in international law in the sense that rights of individual petition are based on an optional clause or optional protocol. See in general, J. Crawford, op. cit. n. 152. It is of course true that the undemocratic features may be somewhat alleviated by measures of democratic control taken at the national level.

without their knowledge.[160] The ever increasing recognition that many 'domestic' problems can only be solved on the international level (environmental issues, nuclear proliferation, refugees, criminal law problems, financial flows, transfer of technology etc.) in recent years has led to a growing body of international law that seeks either to regulate the activities in question or to coordinate national regulation efforts. The resulting erosion of the clear distinction between domestic and international issues has reinforced the power of the executive at the expense of the national legislatures. This expansion of executive power to the detriment of the representative organs, creates a substantial obstacle to the participation by and influence of civil society in affairs that may well directly concern them. This situation is exacerbated by the fact that national parliaments themselves have on the whole no power to ratify or otherwise directly control the decisions of international organisations.[161]

It is in this context that it is clear that international organisations need not only to develop institutions at the international level which will reinforce democracy internally (for example, Office of Fair Elections etc.) but also to enable decision taking by international organisations itself to include organs representing individuals and or national parliaments. The debate on the democratisation of international organisations themselves (an important part of what I term external democracy) has on the whole been a thin one. It has tended to refer to two aspects in particular. First the role which parliamentary assemblies or organs, if established, could play within the decision-making procedure of the particular international organisation itself (4.2.2.1). Second, the role which non state actors could play in that same context (4.2.2.2). The debate has 'thickened' somewhat in recent years with the discussion on the need to move towards what has been termed a 'global civil society' (4.2.2.3).

---

160. See, for example, the Vienna Convention on the Law of Treaties, 23 May 1969: 1155 UNTS 331, Art. 7 (2)(a). See too, J. Crawford, op. cit. n. 152.

161. A treaty establishing and conferring powers on an international organisation will however require the prior ratification by the respective national parliaments. Ratification is the ability to say yes or no to the totality of a treaty as negotiated and not to amend any of its separate parts. See further, Schermers and Blokker, n. 145 op. cit. para. 560. With regard to new 'light' or 'unidentified' international organisations the situation is more nuanced. The Dutch parliament has in particular obtained not inconsiderable rights with regard to decisions taken in the context of the 'third pillar' (justice and home affairs) of the European Union and also with regard to decisions taken by the Executive Commitee established by the Schengen Treaty. See further, D. Curtin and H. Meijers, 'The Principle of Open Government in Schengen and the European Union: Democratic Retrogression?', 32 CML Rev. (1995), pp. 391-442.

4.2.2.1 International parliamentary bodies

It is beyond the scope of this paper to consider the institutional embedding of parliamentary bodies at the international level in any great detail. Suffice it for present purposes to recall that the creation of parliamentary organs to control the decision-making process of international organisations is an almost exclusively European endeavour and dates from the postwar years.[162] Other than the European Parliament of the EC, the most important parliamentary organs are the Parliamentary Assembly of the Council of Europe, the Consultative Interparliamentary Council of Benelux and the Parliamentary Assembly of the Western European Union.[163] In addition the European Economic Area has a parliamentary organ (the Joint Parliamentary Organ) as does the OSCE.[164] All of these organs, with the sole exception of the EC European Parliament, are composed of the members of national parliaments. In terms of functions, Schermers and Blokker, conclude to the effect that:

'As a rule, international parliamentary organs do not play a decisive role in international organisations. They offer an opportunity for *mutual consultation and cooperation between members of parliaments*. This may be very useful but it does not transform international parliamentary organs into real parliaments.'[165]

The exception is of course the EC European Parliament, which is relevant in the context of the European Union. The conclusion with regard to all other parliamentary organs is that none of the parliamentary organs which have been established at the international level exercise anything remotely resembling substantial control over the executive organs of such organisations. They do not in any way therefore redress the executive empowerment entailed by the increasing

---

162. See, H. Schermers and N. Blokker, op. cit. n. 145 at para. 564. They point out that the only exception is the ILO (1919) which included participation in decision-making by representatives of the workers and employers. See also, E. Lochner, 'A Comparative Study of Certain European Parliamentary Assemblies', 4 *European Yearbook* (1956), p. 150 and H-H Lindemann, 'Parliamentary Assemblies, International', 5 EPIL (1983), p. 228.

163. See further, H. Schermers and N. Blokker, op. cit. n. 145.

164. See further, R.S. Oliver, 'The OSCE Parliamentary Assembly', *Helsinki Monitor* (1996), No. 1, p. 42.

165. Op. cit. at para 576. Authors emphasis.

'internationalisation' of previously domestic issues. Any effective redress must thus come from the national parliamentary (and judicial) level.[166]

4.2.2.2 Non state actors

What we do see emerging in relation to an increasing number of international organisations is varying degrees of recognition of the fact that states are no longer the *sole* sources of international legal norms nor the sole initiators of internationally recognised claims. We have individuals as petitioners on bodies such as the Human Rights Committee of the Covenant on Political and Civil Rights. We have non-governmental organisations which have been accorded consultative status by the United Nations and the Council of Europe.[167] We have NGO attendance at international diplomatic conferences with increasing frequency.[168] We have nongovernmental organisations playing an increasingly important role in international judicial proceedings, primarily as *amicus curiae*.[169] And we must not forget the rising significance of the sub-state actor

---

166. See, in general, J.G. Brouwer et al. *Parlement en Buitenlands Beleid* (Zwolle, 1993) and A. Cassese, *Parliamentary Control over Foreign Policy. Legal Essays.* (Alphen aan de Rijn, 1980). See also, P. Everts, *Laat Dat Maar Aan Ons Over! Democratie, Buitenlands Beleid en Vrede* (Leiden, 1996).

167. See further, D. Otto, op. cit. n. 134. See also, R. Brett, 'The Contribution of NGO's to the Monitoring and Protection of Human Rights in Europe: an Analysis of the Role and Access of NGO's to the Intergovernmental Organisations' in A. Bloed et al. (eds.) *Monitoring Human Rights in Europe* (Deventer, 1993), p. 121. See also, P. Willetts (ed.), *The Conscience of the World: the Influence of NGO's in the UN system* (Washington D.C., 1996); Th. G. Weiss and L. Gordenker (eds.), *NGO's, the UN and Global Governance* (Boulder, 1996); P.J. Nelson, *The World Bank and NGO's* (London, 1995).

168. See, in general, L. Elliott, 'International Conference Diplomacy and the Changing Role of NGO's', unpublished manuscript, Australian National University.

169. See, in general, D. Shelton, 'The Participation of Nongovernmental Organisations in International Judicial Proceedings', 88 AJIL (1994) p. 611. See also specifically with regard to the European Convention on Human Rights, O. De Schutter, 'Sur l'Emergence de la Société Civile en Droit International: le Rôle des Associations devant la Cour Européenne des Droits de l'Homme', 7 EJIL (1996) p. 372; M.A. Nowicki, 'NGO's before the European Commission and the Court of Human Rights', 14 *Netherlands Quarterly of Human Rights* (1996) p. 289 and J.P. Loof, 'Amicus curiae in Straatsburg: een Rol voor NGO's binnen het EVRM-Toezichtmechanisme', 21-1 NJCM-Bulletin (1996), p. 13.

within international organisations.[170] Clearly, what has been termed the 'quiet revolution' of the emergence of non state actors, a fast evolving concept, as international actors is far from finished.[171]

The most significant examples of the institutionalisation of non state actors are to be found in the United Nations and the Council of Europe. The UN Charter makes one reference to nongovernment organisations (NGO's) in Article 71 which allows that ECOSOC 'may make suitable arrangements for consultation with nongovernmental organisations which are concerned with matters within its competence'.[172] The present arrangements for consultation with NGO's are set out in ECOSOC Resolution 1296 (XLIV) of 27 May 1968 (hereafter Resolution 1296).[173] By 1993 nearly 1000 NGO's had been granted formal consultative status with ECOSOC by way of these arrangements.[174] This form of consultation with NGO's differs from the right of participation without vote which is granted to observers from non-members, liberation movements and specialised agencies.[175] Outside of the Resolution 1296 procedure there are a plethora of UN-NGO relationships, governed by a broad range of formal and informal procedures.[176] The best known and probably the most far reaching is the role played by NGO's in relation to UN intergovernmental

---

170. In the European Union we not only have the Committee of the Regions but we also have the possibility that sub-state ministers can replace national ministers at Council meetings in appropriate instances. See further in general, J.J. Hesse, (ed.) *Regions in Europe. The Institutionalisation of the Committee of Regions* (Baden-Baden, 1995/96).

171. See, I. Mogami, 'The United Nations System as an Unfinished Revolution', 15 *Alternatives* (1990) p. 177. See also, J. Schramm (ed.), *The Role of Non-governmental Organisations in the new European Order* (Baden-Baden, 1995).

172. See, B. Simma (ed.), *The Charter of the United Nations* (Oxford, 1995), annotation of Article 71, p. 902.

173. In February 1993 ECOSOC established an open ended working group to update, if necessary, its arrangements for consultation with NGO's and to introduce coherent rules to regulate the participation of NGO's in international conferences organised by the UN. ESC res. 1993/80.

174. See, *General Review of Arrangements for Consultations with Non-Governmental Organisations: Report of the Secretary General, UN ESCOR,* UN Doc. E/AC. 70/1994/5 (1994). See further, D. Otto. op. cit. n. 134 and H. Schermers and N. Blokker, op. cit. n. 145 at para. 189 et seq.

175. See, H. Schermers and N. Blokker, op. cit. n. 145 at para. 189.

176. See further, D. Otto, op. cit. n. 134.

conferences in particular in recent years. These developments peaked with the open accreditation processes of the 1992 UN conference on Environment and Development (UNCED) which formally recognised the participation of some 1500 NGO's.[177]

Most specialised agencies of the UN and the Council of Europe grant consultative status to NGO's in much the same way as the ECOSOC.[178] At present consultative status to the Council of Europe is held by 356 organisations.[179] Furthermore, a permanent structure of cooperation between the Council of Europe and NGO's has gradually been established, comprising a Plenary Conference, a Liaison Committee and the Parliamentarian /NGO Joint Committee.[180]

4.2.2.3 The move towards global civil society?

In recent years, there has been renewed stress put on democracy as a value, even a dominant value, in the field of political science, which had its reflection in the international relations sphere. It can be said that at the international level also concern for democracy as a principle has deepened. The political science literature criticising liberal democracy for being unduly formalistic and for not encouraging a more formative politics has also known its counterpart at the international level. This has resulted in particular in the emphasis laid in recent years on the role which a so-called 'international civil society' could have in the context of the democratisation of international relations.[181] International civil society in this sense refers essentially to the networks, movements and organisations of nonprofit interest groups which form to assert interests, identities or causes outside state based and controlled political institutions. The idea is that such nonstate groupings should be enabled to participate in international legal processes as reflective of a multilayered, multinational and participatory identity of transnational citizens.[182] It

---

177. See, D. Otto, op. cit. n. 134 at p. 118.

178. Basic rules governing the relations between the Council of Europe and NGO's have been adopted by Res. (72) 35 of the Committee of Ministers.

179. YIO 1994/95, vol I, at pp. 328-330.

180. See further, H. Schermers and N. Blokker, op.cit n. 145 at para. 195.

181. See in particular, M. Walzer (ed.), *Towards a Global Civil Society* (Oxford, 1995); World Alliance for Citizen Participation (CIVICUS), *Citizens. Strengthening Global Civil Society* (Washington, 1994) and D. Otto, op. cit. n. 134.

182. See, D. Archibugi and D. Held, *Cosmopolitan Democracy* (Oxford, 1995).

manifests the force of a common interest that is more than the aggregate of separate national interests.[183] International or global civil society is seen as a vast, shifting web of interconnections and alliances involving multidimensional human identities.[184] Moreover it is seen as the international counterpart to civil society (nonprofit and nongovernmental) within nation-states which interacts with and exercises a countervailing power on markets and governments.[185]

A commitment to the development of international participatory democracy would seek to ensure that nongovernmental organisations assume in the future an essential, independent status in international affairs that is not confined to mere 'consultation'. The idea would rather be that NGO's could form a vital link between the empowerment of the local and the global structures of governance. Of course the issue of the accountability of NGO's to their constituencies in civil society would need to be assured but further consideration of this and other important aspects are beyond the scope of the present paper.[186] The Commission on Global Governance expresses the challenge which lies ahead as follows:

'A major challenge for the international community is to create the public-private partnerships that enable and encourage non state actors to offer their contributions to effective global governance. Incorporating a multitude of diverse partners into the management of common affairs will be an exceedingly complex affair. Existing institutional variety suggests that a mix of processes and procedures will be required. Systems for collecting information and sharing intelligence, for debating options, for performing specific tasks and for making and implementing decisions will have to be customised according to the issue as well as the interests and skills of the people and institutions concerned.'[187]

---

183. See, D. Otto, op. cit. n. 134.

184. D. Otto, op. cit. n. 134.

185. See further, L.M. Salomon and H.K. Anheier, *The Emergent Sector. An Overview* (Baltimore, 1994).

186. See further, D. Curtin, 'The European Union, Civil Society and Participatory Democracy', *Collected Courses of the Academy of European Law*, Florence, 1996, forthcoming.

187. *Our Global Neighbourhood* (Oxford, 1995), p. 255.

5. The European Union: Technocracy not Democracy

5.1 Introduction

The above discussion with regard to international organisations other than the European Union has shown that the concept of democracy and democratic politics has received relatively little attention and institutionalisation at that level. The debate on giving more content to what may be called a kind of 'international' or 'external' democracy and in particular the attempt to conceptualise a 'global civil society' and its institutionalisation remains fairly utopian at the present moment in time. Even if a trend towards a new internationalism can be detected[188] in the blurring of the distinctions between international and domestic issues and the increasing resolution of previously 'domestic' issues at the international level this has on the whole not been matched by any serious attempt to inject more democratic decision-making methods at the international level. The problem is that the net effect of internationalisation of previously 'domestic' issues is more executive empowerment, since the executive represents the unitary state on the external plane. But on the whole the 'democratic deficit' has not been so glaring with regard to the activity of international organisations other than the EU for the simple reason that they do not directly usurp national legislative power. It follows that the public realm of politics as such has remained within the bounds of the nation-state and is largely unaffected by the functioning of these international organisations.

It is in this context that the case of the European Union is quite unique in the circle of international organisations. Not just because of the daring ambition of its original purpose and the manner in which this took form. This story is well known and I am not going to rehearse it in this paper. Instead I will focus on a less well known tale, that of the dramatic effect of European integration over the years on the public realm of politics within the constituent Member States. The veil of internal politics has not only been lifted, it has been partly shredded. To put it another way: decision-making previously within the purely national domain has been partly taken out of the public realm of politics by virtue of the shift

---

188. See, in particular, P. Tangney, 'The New Internationalism: the Cession of Sovereign Competences to Supranational Organisations and Constitutional Change in the United States and Germany', 21 *Yale Journal of International Law* (1996), p. 395; J.W. Head, 'Supranational Law: How the Move Toward Multilateral Solutions is Changing the Character of International Law', 42 *Kansas Law Review* (1994), p. 605.

in the locus of decision-making to the European level.[189] This is an effect which cooperation in the arena of other international organisations simply has not had. It of course has everything to do with the specific nature of the European integration process and the fact that a significant section of the law adopted is (hierarchically superior) national law (normative supranationalism[190]). The usurping of national legislative power by the European Community is direct and striking. Even putatively 'intergovernmental' decisions increasingly impose requirements that come very close to harmonisation obligations[191] and leave virtually no discretion to national authorities.

✱ A recent example of the far-reaching nature of intergovernmental commitments in the field of criminal law is the adoption by the EU (in secret conclave and only published more than 18 months later) of a joint initiative with the US Federal Bureau of Investigation(FBI) to introduce a global system for the surveillance of telecommunications - phone calls, e-mails and faxes.[192] The 'requirements' to be placed on network and service providers by the EU to enable the surveillance of communications (and interception by 'law enforcement agencies', an American term not defined in the EU's resolution[193]) are based on 'requirements' drawn up by the FBI in 1992 and 1994.[194] The adoption of new, intrusive, surveillance powers by undefined 'law enforcement agencies' was taken in secret by the EU with no democratic discussion at all in the national parliaments of the EU, not to mind the European Parliament. In the US the equivalent measure went through the full round of the democratic process with an open, public debate. In my view this is a good illustration of the removal of an important and sensitive issue with wide

---

189. R. Dehousse categorises this effect as 'depoliticisation' in: 'European Integration and the Nation-state' in M. Rhodes, P. Heywood and V. Wright (eds.), *Developments in West European Politics* (1996).

190. See, J. Weiler, 'The Community System: the Dual Character of Supranationalism' *Yearbook of European Law* (1981), p. 267.

191. See with regard to intergovernmental decision-making in the field of criminal law, A. Klip, 'Uniestrafrecht is op hol geslagen', *Nederlands Juristenblad*, (1997), p. 663.

192. Council Resolution of 17 January 1995 on the Lawful Interception of Telecommunications, OJ 1996 C 329/1.

193. See, *Statewatch report*, March 1997, p. 3: the presumption is that it covers police, intelligence agencies, customs, tax and immigration agencies.

194. See further, *Statewatch*, ibid.

ranging civil liberties implications from the public realm of politics. It constitutes a silencing of democracy and an abolition of public space. ✦

A real political arena does not exist at the level of the EU. The fact that the European Parliament has acquired more joint decision-making powers in recent years (in particular pursuant to the co-decision and assent procedures) has not eliminated this deficit. The lack of a political arena has many causes, including the lack of European wide public parties, the lack of a European wide media and of a European public sphere (see further, *infra.*). What it boils down to is a lack of emphasis and structural possibility for a public sphere of deliberation on matters of public interest.[195] But there are further aggravating factors, including the fact that the Council, composed of the executives of the Member States, is the main legislator and that its meetings and decisions are substantially shrouded in secrecy. Moreover, the manner in which issues are approached and the bargaining to which issues are subjected contribute to reinforce the technocratic image of the Community. As Renaud Dehousse put it:

'the European political system is primarily seen as a closed shop, with membership confined to experts espousing the defence of national or sectoral interests, and not as a political arena within which different conceptions of the public interest can be aired and discussed'.[196]

The net effect is that the inner sovereignty of the state in terms of the locus and content of political community has been severely damaged. At the same time it has not been replaced. So it is not just that certain decisions have direct effect and must be considered as part of national law, albeit hierarchically superior national law, to be applied by national judges. It is also that the state's role as a political arena, the very essence of what has been understood as the internal sovereignty of the nation-state, has been substantially weakened. This is what I term an 'outside-in' effect.

But more is at stake as a result of European integration than this outside-in effect. There is also an 'inside-out' effect. European integration has given rise to a phenomenon of *functional differentiation*

---

195. See, in general, R. Seidelmann, 'Democracy Building in the European Union: Conditions, Problems and Options' in M. Telo, (ed.) *Démocratie et Construction Européenne* (Brussels, 1995) and T. Meyer, 'European Public Sphere and Societal Politics' in M. Telo (ed.), ibid.

196. See, R. Dehousse, 'Institutional Reform in the European Community: are there Alternatives to the Majoritarian Avenue?', Working Paper, EUI, Florence (1995).

among the institutions of governance on a transnational level, encouraging the creation of *networks* linking the executive agencies, judicial bodies and more recently the legislatures of the Member States of the EU.[197] In addition European integration has reinforced a phenomenon of bureaucratic fragmentation in the sense that coordination of European policies is notoriously dificult in many countries.[198] So the unitary nature of the state externally has been undermined from within and fragmented. This phenomenon is of course in addition to the substantial number of transnational networks of non state actors which also operate in and around the European Union.[199]

The effect of fragmentation of state governance structures as a result of on-going European integration fits with the theory of governance which views the European Union as a multilevel system of governance[200] rather than the more classic international two level process.[201] But the result of the fragmentation of the national institutions of governance and in particular the growth in the size and activities of bureacratic structures has gone hand in hand with a weakening of the structures supposed to control and hold accountable the decision makers.[202] This leads us to what may be called a multiple level 'deficit scenario' which at the same time illustrates the 'depoliticisation' which takes place when decisions are taken at the level of the European Union as compared to purely national decision-making. The deficit scenario illustrates the extent to which democratic decision-making as we know it from the national level (as imperfect and 'thin' as it certainly is) does not exist at the level of European Union decision-making (5.2). The

---

197. See further, R. Dehousse, 'European Integration and the Nation-state' op. cit. n. 189.

198. See, L. Metcalf, 'International Policy Coordination and Public Management Reform', 60 *International Review of Administrative Science* (1994), p. 271 and R. Dehousse, op. cit. n. 189.

199. See, Risse-Kappen, (ed.) *Bringing Transnational Relations back in. Non state Actors, Domestic Structures and International Institutions* (Cambridge, 1995).

200. See, G. Marks, L. Hooghe and K. Blank, *European Integration and the State*, European University Institute, Florence, Working Paper No. RSC 95/7.

201. As argued, for example, by the intergovernmentalists, see, A. Moravcsik, 'Preferences and Power in the European Community; A Liberal Inter-governmentalist Approach', 34 *Journal of Common Market Studies* (1993) p. 473.

202. See, R. Dehousse, op. cit. n. 189.

fundamental corollary is whether it is indeed possible to envisage democracy outwith the nation-state: is there a European *demos* (5.3)?

5.2 The multi-level deficit scenario

European integration has considerably increased the power of (national) administrations while making it much more difficult for national parliaments to exert their powers of control. The classic 'democratic deficit' argument is that the shift in the locus of decision-making (to the EU) has not been matched by a shift in the methods of holding the governors accountable to the people. This can be reduced to the argument that the national parliaments cannot hold their ministers accountable for decisions taken by a qualified majority vote by a college of the Council of Ministers, and the European Parliament does not have the powers (and some would argue the ability or proven track record) to perform a general supervisory task similar to that performed by national parliaments at the national level.[203]

But this classic account of the 'democractic deficit' is too weak a view of the scope and nature of the problem at stake. In fact the problem is much more serious than a lack of parliamentary representation at whatever level should prove most appropriate to the type of decision-making. Coming closer to the heart of the matter, we find there is a further deficit and this time at the level of the *separation of powers* and in particular the enormous empowerment of the *executive* which has been a very concrete result of European integration. This deficit is so ensconced in the entire system of EU governance that it is a difficult task to recapitulate the scope and gravity of the problem in a few short sentences. The tip of the iceberg is the well known fact that the Council, composed of government Ministers, legislates behind closed doors. But the decision-making of this legislative authority is prepared by a massive circus of committees composed of national civil servants and technical experts, they too operating behind closed doors and in virtual secrecy. Pioneering work undertaken by the Rotterdam political scientist, Rinus van Schendelen, has recently shown how pervasive this system is and how in fact a significant number of the Council's decisions are actually taken in all their details by the Council's preparatory committees, simply being rubber stamped as so-called 'A' points on the Councils

---

203. See further, R. Dehousse, (1995), op. cit. n. 189.

Agenda.[204] National civil servants in conclave taking legislative decisions is far removed from even the thinnest notion of democracy as we know it in the nation-states. Neo-absolutism seems a more descriptive term in this context than democracy as a label for the decision-making procedure. Such neo-absolutism is present in a particularly aggravated form in the context of decision-making in the third pillar where the empowerment of the executive and of civil servants has been institutionalised particularly strongly.[205]

Part of the lack of separation of powers is what may be termed a *rule of law deficit*. By this terminology I am referring to the increasingly common tendency, in particular in the field of justice and home affairs, for the Government Ministers acting within the framework of the Council to seek to exclude any independent judicial supervisory mechanism to control and interpret the decisions taken in this field.[206] This has proven to be a very controversial point in practice with certain Member States adopting a strongly dogmatic line to the effect that any involvement whatsoever by the Court of Justice in the interpretation and or resolution of disputes arising in the context of K. 3 conventions would contaminate the intergovernmental nature of decision-making. This attitude has resulted in the practice of including in a separate *optional* protocol to some international agreements a right for the Court of Justice to give preliminary rulings (see, for example, Europol Convention, Customs Information System Convention, Convention on the protection of the financial interest of the EC).[207] This particular rule of law deficit is of course especially serious where what is at stake is legislation or quasi legislation which directly affects the rights and interests of individual citizens.

The ascendency of bureacracy poses a further danger to democracy in that it intensifies secrecy in policy formation, the very antithesis to

---

204. M.P.C.M. van Schendelen, 'The Council Decides. Does the Council Decide?', JCMS (1996), p. 531. and M.P.C.M. van Schendelen, 'EC Committees: Influence Counts more than Legal Powers' in R.H. Pedler and G.F. Schaefer (eds.), *Shaping European Law and Policy. The Role of Committees and Comitology in the Political Process* (Maastricht, 1996), p. 25.

205. See, in general, H. Meijers, (ed.) *Democracy, Migrants and Police in the European Union: The 1996 IGC and Beyond,* (Utrecht, 1997).

206. See, K. Groenendijk, 'The European Court of Justice and the Third Pillar' in H. Meijers (ed.), ibid.

207. See further, D. Curtin and J.F.M. Pouw, 'La Cooperation dans le Domaine de la Justice et des Affaires Intérieures au Sein de l'Union Européenne: une Nostalgie d'avant Maastricht?', *Revue de Marché Unique Europeen*, 3/1995, p. 13.

democracy. Information is and remains the currency of democracy. In the case of the European Union the reason most commonly given for secretive decision-making is related to the efficiency of the decision-making process, in particular taking into account the fact that decision-making in Council bears the hallmarks of negotiated diplomacy more than those of democratic decision-making.[208] But let us not forget that bureacrats use secrecy not only for the sake of efficiency but also to augment their own power. I am reminded of the well known observer of bureacracy who wrote: 'Bureacracy is like sin: we all know something about it, but only those who practise it enjoy it'.[209]

This is not the place to detail the scope and limits of reforms which have taken place with regard to introducing the principle of access to documents at the Union level.[210] But the Union still has a long road to tread to move away from its categorisation as a regime more resembling a totalitarian regime than a democratic one in terms of the secretive nature of its decision-making. The fact that the EU institutions may have started the process of 'modernising' their information policies by acquiring Web pages on the INTERNET and placing on it documents that are in the public domain anyway is clearly not enough.[211] What is ultimately needed is a much more pro-active policy on making freely available documents which form part of the decision-making process itself, including all of its preparatory instances.[212]

To conclude I would relate my analysis of the core deficits of the EU to the perception that the European Community was originally

---

208. See further, D.M. Curtin, 'Betwixt and Between: Democracy and Transparency in the Governance of the European Union' in J.A. Winter et al. (ed.), *Reforming the Treaty on the European Union* (The Hague, 1996), p. 95.

209. B. Chapman, *The Profession of Government* (London, 1959), as quoted in K.I. Meier, *Politics and the Bureacracy* (1979), p. xv.

210. See further, D.M. Curtin, op. cit. n. 208 and P. Birkenshaw, 'Freedom of Information and Open Government: The European Community/Union Dimension', 14 *Government and Information Quarterly* (1997), p. 27.

211. See further, D. Curtin, 'The European Union, Civil Society and Participatory Democracy', op. cit. n. 186.

212. For example on the Internet. How much this remains a vision for the future was witnessed recently by the negative reaction of all the other Member States to the Dutch presidency's intention to place IGC 'non-papers' (discussion documents) on the Internet as they became available. The torpedoing of this innovative initiative led to a Dutch member of the European Parliament placing the same (and more) IGC documents back on the Internet on her own Webpage: http://www.xs4all.nl/~nelvdijk/.

designed to preserve the authority of the nation-state as such and its prosperity.[213] Wealthy and secure citizens of the post-war nation-states, it was surmised, would make happy and contented citizens. The EC's historical mission in this view was to 'save' the nation-state in effect. While I do not disagree with this view in terms of an economic analysis I hope that I have at least succeeded in showing that while the EC may have increased the capacity of the respective nation-states to take effective economic action, at the same time and more subtly the state's role as the only possible political arena safeguarding the implementation of the principle of self-government was being steadily undermined. This fragmentation process was undertaken both from within the state (the separate parts of the *trias politica* and other non state actors involved in transnational relations), and from outside (decision-making within the governance system of the EU itself). Far from having *saved* the system of democracy enshrined with such pain and turbulence in national constitutions, the process of closer European integration embodied in the EU has had the effect of fragmenting and dispersing the legislative power of the individual constituent nation-states. At the same time the excessive empowerment of the executive results in a neo absolutist process of decision-making with dramatic consequences for notions of democracy enshrined at the national level.

5.3 Does a 'demos' exist at the European level?

Given this picture of contemporary gloom and doom then surely the only sensible path is indeed one of national entrenchment? Maybe the Euro sceptics are not such siren voices after all. Isn't any notion of democracy beyond the nation-state at best sheer Utopianism and at worst downright dangerous?

Let me now move the discussion to another level of analysis, that proffered by the highly respectable members of the German Constitutional Court, the *Bundesverfassungsgericht*.[214] Those familar with the subject matter will know that this brings us close to the heart of the problem: given this terrible 'here' which I have sketched for you, where can we possibly *go* with this 'here' as our starting point? Is there a 'there' which can be labelled, for example, 'postnational democracy'? This is the essence of the problem the German Constitutional Court had to grapple with when deciding on the constitutionality of the Maastricht Treaty. Somewhat unkindly, I am going to liken their collective wisdom

---

213. See, A. Milward, *The European Rescue of the Nation-State* (London, 1992).

214. *Brunner* [1994] CMLR 57.

to that of the willy Celt I mentioned earlier. If the 'there' in the sense of some postnational democracy exists at all (which the German Constitutional Court doesn't believe), it can most certainly not be reached by starting from the 'here' and now. Moreover, the 'here' may not be entirely comfortable but what has to be avoided at all costs in their view is any further movement down the road to closer European integration because that would constitute an unacceptable negation of the requirements of a democracy at the national (German) level.

Let's examine their reasoning a little closer: democracy requires a *demos*, a people and a people in this sense can only be understood as an organic ethnically defined whole, a pre-existing *Volk*. On this definition there is of course no *demos* at the European level nor is there any likelihood whatsoever that it will come into being. Thus democracy cannot be constituted at the level of the EU itself but only at the level of the independent Member States. Democracy can only be guaranteed at the nation-state level since historically political identity became nationalised in modern Europe to the point where the equation nationality = (cultural and political) *identity* becomes another sort of social fact or social construction that is taken for granted.[215]

It is apparently a prerogative neither of sex, of nationality nor of profession to wish to cling to tired old shibboleths of bygone eras. I cannot put it in less unequivocal language than that used by Joseph Weiler:

> 'How *sad* ... to observe the *Bundeverfassungsgericht*, faced with the need and historical opportunity, to rethink ... issues in the context of Community and Member State, looking backwards, like Lot's wife, to a polity based on *the tired old ideas of an ethno-culturally homogenous Volk* and the unholy trinity of Volk-Staat-Staatsangehoriger as the exclusive basis for democratic authority and legitimate rule making'.[216]

In any event the German judges conveniently ignored the fact that there is a serious problem *here and now* and not just in the future and not just as

---

215. See, R. Kearney, op. cit. n. 11 at p. 18.

216. J. Weiler, 'The State über alles'. Demos, Telos and the German Maastricht Decision', Harvard Jean Monnet Working Paper 6/95, p. 5. See too, T. Koopmans who also expressed his disappointment with the lack of new thinking in 'Rechter, D-mark en Democratie: het Bundesverfassungsgericht en de Europese Unie', 69 NJB, 25 February 1994, pp. 245, 249. See also, R. de Lange, 'Het Bundesverfassungsgericht over het Verdrag van Maastricht: een nieuwe Solange?', SEW 6 (1994), pp. 418, 434.

a result of any changes which the Treaty of Maastricht may or may not have introduced. The German court implicitly invites us to think of Europe in pre-(nation) state terms. It recalls Einstein's comment that everything has changed but our way of thinking. State-based control techniques cannot suffice for the simple reason that the European Union is *not* a would-be (nation) state, still less a state. It is the pre-state misunderstanding which produces the zero sum relationship between the European Union and the Member State.

I believe that the effort of reimagining political community other than premised on an ethno-culturally homogenous *Volk* is an imperative task. The alternative is not as the Euro sceptic would have us believe that of a perfectly fine status quo where an adequate system of accountability can be assured at the national level. No, the alternative is much more grim and bleak than the often unsophisticated Euro sceptic reaction would have us believe: it is the route of increasingly authoritarian and non participative decision-making, increasingly far removed from the by now entirely alienated citizen.

The challenge of what I term 'postnational democracy' is precisely to attempt to avoid this fate. The potential of developing 'postnational democracy' is as an attempt to visualise a viable political arena at the level of the European Union itself. A political arena designed not to replace the political arena of the nation-state but rather to *supplement* it in very necessary, albeit complementary, ways. It is not a zero sum game, the postnational replacing the national political unit, and 'the winner takes all' kind of scenario. Nor can we deny the very crucial fact that that political identity may be crucially formed at the subnational level, the regional or local level.

It is beyond the scope of this paper to further elaborate the important *subnational* angle but its existence and development goes hand in glove with the postnational level. It is not therefore just a matter of pushing sovereignty and citizenship upwards. The hope for self government lies not in the relocation of sovereignty but in dispersing it.[217] 'The nation-state need not fade away', as Michael Sandel puts it, 'only cede its claim as sole repository of sovereign power and primary object of political allegiance. Different forms of political association would govern different spheres of life and engage different aspects of our identities'.[218]

It is precisely multiperspective interconnectedness which will produce networks of interaction typifying a multilevel polity. What is

---

217. See too, M. Sandel, *Democracy's Discontent*, op. cit. n. 78 at p. 345.

218. Ibid.

emerging therefore is something much less unitary, something much more diffuse than the nation-state. Some would argue, the first political and constitutional order to be created in the postmodern era.[219] The first postmodern polity in effect. Stephen Hawking would feel at home with the fragmentation, overlapping and indeterminacy implied by postmodernism in this context.

6. Postnational Democracy and the European Union

6.1 What's in a name?

Why the terminology postnational?[220] Isn't everything 'post' something these days, the catchword of modern times? Post-communism, post-liberalism, post-sovereignty, post-modernity. Why add postnational to the list? And what is its relationship to 'supranational', 'international' and 'transnational'?

The 'post' in 'postnational' is meant to express the idea that democracy is possible beyond the nation-state: what is being left behind in terms of political identity is the link with nationalism in the sense of cultural integration. The term 'postnational' expresses the idea that the link implied by nationalism between cultural integration and political integration can be prised open. But first one has to summarise the

---

219. See, I. Ward, 'Identity and Difference: The European Union and Postmodernism' in J. Shaw and G. More, *New Legal Dynamics of European Union* (Oxford, 1995), pp. 15, 26. See too, R. Cooper, *The Post-Modern State and the World Order* (London, 1996).

220. I don't claim any exclusivity for the term: it has been used by a few other authors in connection with the conceptualisation of citizenship beyond the nation-state, but little attention has been given to its distinctive characteristics and in particular how it must be distinguished from 'supranational', 'international' etc. See, for example, Y. Soysal, *Limits of Citizenship. Migrants and Postnational Membership in Europe* (Chicago, 1994); M. Feldblum, 'Changing Strategies of Citizenship in Contemporary Europe: National, Neonationalist and Postnationalist Strategies', unpublished manuscript, January 1996 and J. Shaw, 'Citizenship of the Union: Towards Post-National Membership' *Collected Courses of the Academy of European Law*, Florence (1995), forthcoming. The earliest and most comprehensive use of the term that I have traced is by J.-M. Ferry in 1992: 'Pertinence du Postnational' in J. Lenoble and N. Dewandre, *L'Europe au Soir du Siecle. Identité et Démocratie.* (Paris, 1992). See also, F-R. Martin, 'L'Europe et la Problematique de la Culture: Cosmopolitisme, Etat-nation, Democratie' in *L'Union Européenne. Droit, Politique, Démocratie* (Paris, 1996), p. 267.

structural function of nationalism as providing the ideological glue that defined a relatively circumscribed group of people and unified them around a set of shared institutions and practices that were informed by a common political culture and were sovereign over a well defined territory.[221] The resultant *identity* imparted a special function of inclusion and exclusion.[222]

'National identity' in its distinctive sense is thus an identity which derives from membership in a 'people' the fundamental characteristic of which is that it is defined as a 'nation'. In other words, as Gellner put it, nationalism, is defined as the striving to endow a culture with its own political roof, and not more than one political roof at that.[223] So it's not just a question of national unity but of the congruence of national unity with political identity.[224] Political community, loyalty, accountability and legitimacy were tied in this way to state power and authority.

The *postnational* idea on the contrary is premised precisely on the separation of politics and culture, of nationality and citizenship. The significance of the expression 'postnational identity' is precisely the 'dépassement' of the nationalist principle as defined by Gellner. This is the defining difference with supranationalism because the latter is premised on the idea that the nation-state can be recreated at a larger geo-institutional scale, '*super*-nationalism' which does not eliminate the understandings behind nationalism as such but simply makes a shift in scale.[225] The *postnational* idea on the contrary is about separating out a number of our most elided concepts cherished within the nation-state. It presupposes that national (cultural) plurality can coexist alongside with political unity. In other words the 'nation' when extracted from the hard core of the 'state' with its functions of of defence, money, borders etc.

---

221. See, R. Bellamy and D. Castiglione, 'The Communautarian Ghost in the Cosmopolitan Machine: Constitutionalism, Democracy, and the Reconfiguration of Politics in the New Europe' in R. Bellamy (ed.) *Constitutionalism, Democracy and Sovereignty: American and European Perspectives* (Aldershot, 1996), p. 111.

222. See, R. Kearney, op. cit. n. 11 at p. 9.

223. E. Gellner, *Nations and Nationalism*, op. cit. n 56. at p. 43

224. See, J. Ferry, op. cit. n. 220 at p. 41.

225. On the specifics of 'supranational democracy' see the excellent studies by M. Telo: 'Démocratie internationale et démocratie supranationale en Europe' in M. Telo (ed.) *Démocratie et Construction Européenne* (Brussels, 1995), p. 1 and M. Telo and P. Magnette, 'Les remises en cause de l'Europe politique depuis la chute du mur de Berlin: vers une démocratie supranationale et post-fédérale' in M. Telo and P. Magnette, *Repenser l'Europe* (Brussels, 1996), p. 7.

can take on a 'wobbly shape' of a more flexible *cultural* process independent of political institutions.[226]

And the corollary is that in terms of political identity, the requisite *demos* to enable a democracy to exist can be constituted other than in the organic ethnic terms of the German Constitutional Court.

6.2 Alternative visions of democracy and the European Union

The *demos* required by the postnational-European-construct can potentially be understood in *different* ways leading to different conceptualisations and potentialities for Europe. In any event, it seems clear that if we wish to access a radical alternative vision of *demos,* then we will need to explore the full potential of alternative conceptual visions. German sociology and political theory has itself come up with a challenging concept in this regard, Constitutional Patriotism, which has been defined as 'the ability to identify with the political order and the principles stemming from the Basic Law'.[227] In this vision it is the political culture which must serve as the common denominator for a constitutional patriotism which simultanously sharpens an awareness of the multiplicity of the different forms of life which coexist in a multicultural society (unity in diversity). This patriotism towards the Constitution can only be deployed once culture and politics are more separated than they are at present in the nation-state. The emphasis in this model on a common core of civic values could potentially prove apposite in the case of the EU as it is evolving. At the very least it is worth exploring this issue further in the future.

Another distinguishing feature of the kind of democracy envisaged at the postnational level is the *political philosophy* informing it. The kind of democracy which underlines postnational democracy is 'thick' democracy as opposed to its 'thinner' nation-state counterpart. Postnational democracy seeks to link in with alternative theories of democracy, and in particular those advocating a more *deliberative* notion of democracy than that implied and practised under a purely

---

226. See, E. Hobsbawn, *Nations and Nationalism since 1780* (Cambridge, 1990).

227. See, J. Habermas, 'Conscience historiques et identité posttraditionelle. L'Orientation a l'Ouest de la RFA', in *Ecrits Politiques. Culture, Droit, Histoire* (Paris, 1990), pp. 225, 233. See too, his 'Citizenship and National Identity' op. cit. n. 10 and 'The European Nation-state. Its Achievements and its Limitations. On the Past and Future of Sovereignty and Citizenship', 9 *Ratio Juris* (1996), pp. 125, 133-137. See also, J. Weiler, 'The State über alles', op. cit. n. 216 at p. 27. and F.R. Martin, op. cit. n. 220 at pp. 284-285.

representative model. It also recognises the crucial potential which a non-governmental space has to play in injecting more deliberation into representative process. This alternative perception of democracy relies on the insight of deliberative theorists who perceive *will formation processes* as essential for democracy. It therefore emphasises active dialogic participation, rather than the intermittently passive procedural participation -voting- as the key for democratising decision-making processes.[228] Such participation is on-going, not periodic. The model of deliberative democracy thus does not hinge on the assumptions of macro-subjects, like the 'people' of a particular community, but on anonymously interlinked discourses or flows of communication.[229]

The deliberative ideal also starts from the premise that political preferences will conflict and that the purpose of democratic institutions must be to resolve this conflict. But it envisages this occuring through an open and uncoerced discussion of the issue at stake with the aim of arriving at an agreed judgment.[230] Whereas a liberal vision of democracy stresses the importance of giving due weight to each individual's distinct preferences, the deliberative view relies upon a person's capacity to be swayed by rational arguments and to lay aside particular interests and opinions in deference to overall fairness and the common interest of the collectivity. The common good in this vision is categorically different from an accommodation of private individual preferences as the goal of government policy.

It can be argued that the liberal vision of freedom lacks the *civic resources* to sustain self government and makes it ill equipped to cope

---

228. See further, J. Habermas, *Between Facts and Norms. Contributions to a Discourse Theory of Law and Democracy* (Massachusetts, 1996) and C. Taylor, 'Liberal politics and the public sphere' in A. Etzioni, *New Communautarian Thinking. Persons, Virtues, Institutions and Communities* (Charlottesville, 1995), p. 183. From this perspective politics is understood as an ongoing transformative dialogue among citizens. In such a dialogue, citizens confront one another, challenging their 'linguistically encoded self-understandings, sensibilities and ways of knowing': see, F. Michelman, 'Personal but not split: Radin versus Rorty', 63 Cal.L.Rev. (1990) p. 1783.

229. See, J. Habermas, ibid. at p. 11.

230. See further, J. Cohen, 'Deliberation and Democratic Legitimacy' in A. Hamlin and P. Petit (eds.) *The Good Polity* (Oxford, 1989); B. Manin, 'On Legitimacy and Political Deliberation', *Political Theory* 15 (1987), pp. 338-68; J. Drysek, *Discursive Democracy*, (Cambridge, 1990); D. Millar, 'Deliberative Democracy and Social Choice' in D. Held (ed), *Prospects for Democracy* (Oxford, 1993), p. 74.

with the 'sense of disempowerment that affects our public life'.[231] Informing the people's discretion in a situation where they are only active at the moment elections are held is arguably not nearly enough. Many are those who advocate the revival of a more *formative politics,* a politics that cultivates in citizens the qualities of character that self-government requires. It encourages people not merely to express their political opinions but to *form* those opinions through debate in public settings.[232] Civic republican political theory, for example, perceives freedom in terms of more active citizen participation in politics, the deliberation with fellow citizens about the common good and the active shaping of the destiny of the political community.[233] The 'creative' aspect of deliberation must be emphasised: public values are 'forged' through the act of public participation, created through common deliberation and common action. 'Civic virtue' becomes a positive experience of moral freedom.[234]

The idea of a more deliberative politics, of more active citizen participation does not need to be perceived as an *alternative* to liberal democracy's representative government but rather as a necessary and valuable *supplement* to it. The attempt is rather to rediscover the importance of *deliberation in representative democracy* amongst the citizens, amongst citizens and representatives and amongst the representatives themselves. The idea is that through deliberation based on citizen participation, representative democracy will be able to realise its full potential.[235]

---

231. See, M.J. Sandel, op. cit. n. 78 at p. 6.

232. Ibid.

233. See, for example, F. Michelman, 'The Supreme Court, 1985 Term-Traces of Self-Government', 100 Harv. L. Rev. (1986), p. 4 and F. Michelman, 'Law's Republic', 97 Yale L.J. (1988) p. 1493; C. Sunstein, 'Participation, Public Law and Venue Reform', 49 U.Chi.L.Rev. (1982) p. 976 and C. Sunstein, 'Beyond the Republican Revival', 97 Yale L.J. (1988), p. 1539. See, generally Symposium, 'The Republican Civic Tradition', 97 Yale L.J. (1988), p. 1493. See also, P.P. Craig, *Public Law and Democracy in the United Kingdom and the United States of America* (Oxford, 1990).

234. See, in general, R.D. Putnam, *Making Democracy Work. Civic Traditions in Modern Italy* (Princeton, 1993). See also, C. Offe, *Der Tunnel am Ende des Lichts* (Frankfurt, 1994).

235. See, J. Stewart, 'Democracy and Local Government' in P. Hirst and S. Khilnani, *Reinventing Democracy* (Oxford, 1996), pp. 48-49.

6.3 A European political public sphere

The core is a political public sphere which enables citizens to take positions at the same time on the same topics of the same relevance.[236] It must be embedded in a freedom valuing political culture and supported by a liberal associational structure.[237] The role of the political parties is then to mediate between the spheres of informal public communications and the more institutionalised deliberation and decision processes. The public sphere generates a *public opinion* which arises out of a common discussion even though the participants never meet in a single place and moment.[238]

The development of a European public sphere is crucial to the conceptualisation of democracy at the postnational level. As of now it is generally recognised that the European Union is far from constituting what could properly be called a common European public sphere.[239] Large parts of the European issues under discussion in the EU decision-making institutions are not discussed in public and, if they are, it is in almost all cases in a fragmented way, more or less separated within the national public spheres. Thomas Meyer has put the problem as follows:

'... there is nothing like a European wide discourse of the key issues of the European agenda which connects the arguments and counter arguments, competing opinions and interpretations on a European scale, so that arguments from various national, regional or sectoral quarters of the EU can regularly, continually and in a sufficiently structured manner meet and form something like a European public opinion.'[240]

---

236. See, J. Habermas, 'Remarks on Dieter Grimm's "Does Europe Need a Constitution"', 3 *European Law Journal* (1995), pp. 303, 306.

237. Ibid.

238. See, C. Taylor, 'Liberal Politics and the Public Sphere' in A. Etzioni (ed.), *New Communautarian Thinking. Persons, Virtues, Institutions and Communities* (Charlottesville, 1995), pp. 183, 202.

239. See, T. Meyer, 'European Public Sphere and Societal Politics' in M. Telo, *Democratie et Construction Européenne* (Brussels, 1995), pp. 123, 126. See also, M. Martinello, 'Citizenship of the European Union. A Critical View' in R. Baubock, *From Aliens to Citizens. Redefining the Status of Immigrants in Europe* (Aldershot, 1994), p. 29.

240. T. Meyer, ibid. at p. 126.

A European wide integrated public sphere entails public communication transcending the boundaries of the up until now limited national public spheres. This will include a European wide civil society with interest associations, non-governmental organisations, citizens' movements etc. interconnected with but with some separate existence from the national public spheres.[241] It is precisely in this respect that something new is afoot: a process of rehabilitation of a genuinely non-governmental civic space at the European level has in my view actually commenced. The politicisation of a non-governmental civic space at the level of EU is witnessed *inter alia* by the unprecedented involvement and activity of the non-governmental sector at the European level on the fringes of the current Intergovernmental process.[242] Part of the process is the nesting of smaller (national and local) public spheres in a larger (European) one. It is also indicative of a process of self mobilisation and self constitution. Sucessful common action can bring a sense of empowerment and also strengthen identification with the political community.

The emergence of civil society at the European level, albeit still nascent, is potentially a significant factor in the construction from below of a public sphere worth its name. The start of self constitution is the realisation that participatory democracy has to grow bottom up. It must come from below, from the people, from groups of people dedicated to the disinterested search for the public interest of society.[243] We must

---

241. See too, J. Habermas, op. cit. n. 236 at p. 306.

242. See further for the scope and details of such activity, D. Curtin, 'The European Union, Civil Society and Participatory Democracy' op. cit. n. 186. In total hundreds of NGO's and pressure groups of all types have submitted written observations to the IGC itself on desirable changes as well as participating in the public hearings for civil society organised by the European Parliament in preparation of its own observations to the IGC. Moreover some 50 organisations representing civil society have joined forces at the initiative of the International European Movement as a *Civil Society Forum* meeting in parallel with the formal IGC, a kind of 'fringe' conference to the real diplomatic conference, a phenomenon which has become such an integral part of the United Nations Conference landscape in recent years.

243. See too, B. Barber, 'Three Challenges to Reinventing Democracy' in P. Hirst and S. Khilnani, op. cit. n. 235 at p. 144. The argument is sometimes made that NGO's etc. active at the European level are motivated by a *negative* desire to prevent the European level of decision-making destroying what has been achieved at the national level. This is undoubtedly the case. But it is striking how many of these groups and associations are genuinely reflecting as to the novel configuration which must emerge at the European level, one which respects the values held dear by these public interest groups.

not look to governments or bureaucrats to make these democratic transformations; participatory democracy, like active citizenship,[244] cannot be imposed top down.

Under a more deliberative theory of democracy the role of civil society or more specifically of a non-governmental civic sphere is not necessarily something prior to politics but can also function as a seedbed for citizenship in a transition to democracy context. But it then follows that the clear boundary between the institutionalised political system and public sphere has to be relaxed. The civil society sphere has to play its role in widening and expanding the public debate. Further lines of inquiry clearly include study of the kinds of groups involved at present, the extent to which they belong to the 'voluntary' or 'public interest' sector, the manner in which the latter has to be defined and the extent to which their internal constitution itself respects the democratic principle.[245]

At the same time, it is vital that the top down structures (the IGC, for example) recognise the vitality and significance of the emergent civil society and that they too seek ways in which some form of institutionalisation can take place in the long run. The demands of civil society regarding its own institutionalisation at the EU level are twofold, at least in the specific context of an emerging seedbed for EU citizenship. *First*, the right of association, not in the classic sense of the right to form trade unions but rather the right for European wide organisations and groups to constitute themselves at the European wide level rather than under the law and subject to the tax and legal regime of one single Member State.[246] Formal legal recognition would underline the importance of these active citizens with a public interest perspective on

---

244. See further, B.J. Turner, 'Outline of a Theory of Citizenship', 24 *Sociology* (1990), p. 189. 'Passive' citizenship is developed 'from above' by the state through the granting of rights, and 'active citizenship' from below by the citizens through their participation in various social movements. On the interface between EU citizenship and civil society see further, D. Curtin, 'The European Union, Civil Society and Participatory Democracy', op. cit. n. 186.

245. See further, D. Curtin, 'The European Union, Civil Society and Participatory Democracy', op. cit., n. 186.

246. See, for example, the submissions made by European Citizen Action Service (ECAS) to the IGC: *European Citizenship. Giving Substance to Citizens' Europe in a Revised Treaty. A Memorandum for the ECAS Hotline* (Brussels, 1996). ECAS is the result of a coalition of citizens associations called VOICE (Voluntary Organisations in a Citizens' Europe) and the distillation of over 300 positions of NGO's which have given evidence to the European Parliament's Committee on Institutional Affairs.

the issues being debated within the formal decision-making process itself.

A separate question is the way in which such European wide public interest associations should be enabled to participate in the EU decision-making process itself.[247] Should this include a formal right of *consultation* along the lines of what the social partners obtained in the social policy field or analous to NGO consultations in other international organisations? Or should there simply be easier access to relevant *information* so that they can more effectively represent the public interest on specific issues to parliamentarians, either national or European? In other words the idea would be that more structured citizen participation would *inform* but not determine the process of representative government. The latter approach would involve a rediscovery of the importance of deliberation in representative democracy by means of a more open and uncoerced discussion of the issue at stake with the aim of arriving at an agreed judgment. As has already been stated this should not be perceived as a threat to representative democracy but rather as a necessary complement to it. The exact institutional configuration of a more participatory role for 'civil society' in the European Union is complex and requires detailed further study.

6.4 Information technology and the re-imagination of political identity

A transformation or re-imagination of our shared understandings may well be made possible in part by the advent of advanced *information technology* which is changing the nature of the physical world we live in, a physical world in which borders are rapidly becoming irrelevant. I am fascinated by the potential that the new cyberspace offers in this theoretical context in two respects. First, as a means of communication facilitating a genuine social dialogue among the citizens. Part of this issue is of course wider availability of information relating to the formal political process itself, and the potential of cyberspace is enormous albeit still radically underdeveloped in this respect. Digital networks potentially transform the way we create, exchange and access information as well as the way we interact in private and in public. It is this transformation of social dialogue which can be of such significance to democratic

---

247. See further, P.P. Craig, 'Democracy and Rulemaking within the EC: an Empirical and Normative Assessment', 3 *European Law Journal* (1997), p. 105. See also, D. Curtin, 'The European Union, Civil Society and Participatory Democracy' op. cit. n. 186.

theory.[248] Digitisation may open up social dialogue to more people by enhancing the accessibility of means of creation and communication. It may thus allow individuals to access the deliberative process as active participators rather than as mere passive receivers of messages. It may also enhance the ability of individuals to access relevant information that may be crucial for will formation purposes.[249]

But secondly, and crucially, when one refers to a postnational context, we must think of the link between the new means of communication offered by cyberspace and the exercise of imagining 'communities' where borders are irrelevant. Let me very briefly explain the evolution over time which has taken place in this regard. In so called primitive societies, the link or social glue was provided by a storyteller. In Vargas Llosa's remarkable novel *The Storyteller* he describes the almost mythical figure of a storyteller moving through the Amazonian forest, linking different fragments of a people in geographically remote pockets of Peru. Word of mouth and the physical travel of the storyteller himself were the critical elements in weaving together a sense of community, of belonging, of a continuing and cohesive narrative.

The advent of the Gutenburg printing press in the 16th century was crucial in enabling 'national' communities to be imagined and national identity to emerge. The cultural anthropologist Benedict Anderson has provided a powerful account of how it was only in the modern era that it was made possible for people from diverse locales to 'imagine' themselves part of a single community. In Anderson's view the spread of print media through the capitalist market permitted an unprecedented mode of apprehending time that entailed the ability to imagine the simultanous existence of one's co-nationals.

The next stage in this scale is the potential provided by the new world of cyberspace which makes geographical borders irrelevant. My suggestion is that we begin to explore ways in which digitisation can facilitate an effort of *imagination* transcending those of national borders and thus have potential in terms of *facilitating* the construction of a postnational political identity. Opinion forming associations which specialise in issues and contributions and are generally designed to generate influence, belong to the civil society infrastructure of a public sphere dominated by the mass media. Jurgen Habermas has termed this the political public sphere, 'a communication structure rooted in the

---

248. See, N. Elkin-Koren, 'Cyberlaw and Social Change: A Democratic Approach to Copyright Law in Cyberspace', 14 *Cardoza Arts and Entertainment Law Review* (1996) pp. 215, 218 et seq.

249. See, N. Elkin-Koren, ibid.

lifeworld through the associational network of civil society'.[250] This is potentially the modern day counterpart to the public sphere constituted by print capitalism which shaped a common sphere of communication leading to imagined communities of readers.

Of course I immediately anticipate reactions to the effect that the new technology is elitist. This is true but does not mean that we have to dismiss its potential out of hand. Let's not forget: so too in its time was the printing press and look what it had become by the twentieth century. What we have to do is to look towards the future, the next decade or so, and the situation where approximately 90% of the population will be connected to Internet, an Internet as easy to operate as a telephone. It is largely a question of time.

7. Concluding Remarks

The European Community has been regarded as a crisis system almost from the very beginning. The fact that the progress of integration implies intensified crisis is not in itself call for alarm.[251] The most that can be said is maybe that the nature of the crisis has changed somewhat, from operational stress to one with more of a basis in fundamental existential questions. Given the life phase of the EC as such, in its fourth decade, this is of course not so surprising. We know from systems theory, from biology and from the study of human psychology that the very survival of a system includes the concept of *change*, namely the capacity of a system to *respond* to stress.

What does give rise to concern is the fact that the existential crisis of the EU, if we can term it that, is too easily and too superficially glossed over. All effort is directed to what may be described as *a systems maintenance exercise.*[252] The latter exercise which I think is personified by the current IGC is weighted inevitably with the notion of salavaging the *existing* patterns of relationships. In other words, preservation of the existing *status quo* with a certain number of minor alterations, a tinkering exercise in terms of technique. This exercise does not address any real attention or credence to the need to address the existential dilemmas in order to help the system genuinely to respond to stress, and proceed a more solid basis. It is what might be termed the very *life processes* of the

---

250. *Between Facts and Norms*, op. cit. n. 228.

251. See, L.N. Lindberg, 'Integration as a Source of Stress on the European Community System', *International Organisation*, (1966), pp. 233, 235.

252. See, D. Easton, *A Framework for Political Analysis*, (Englewood Cliffs, N.J., 1965), p. 88.

system which require urgent attention if the system is to continue to grow organically.

The attempt to develop what has been called postnational democracy is an effort to conceptualise a viable political entity beyond the nation-state. It is also an attempt to begin to challenge our existing nation-state (pre)conceptions.[253] The effort is premised on the belief that there is no option of simply stopping the clock and returning to the safety and familiarity of the nation-state. A bunker mentality denies the fact that an essential part of decision-making transcends borders in the modern world. Bunker politics results in an authoritarian here and now and it will result in an authoritarian tomorrow.

The challenge is rather to attempt to conceptualise a viable political arena at the level where decisions are actually taken, be they local, regional, state or beyond. The conclusion is that no mechanistic answer is possible. The more fragmentary, fluid, indeterminate future of Stephen Hawking beckons. The nation-state as cultural demos is the common knowledge which is under challenge as we move towards the next Millennium. But the essence of constitutive politics is the deliberative process of evolving new common worlds in new media; it may lack the fixity of what we have lost, but it promises a richer texture.

One final thought on footbridges to the Millenium and the Enlightenment process in Europe. As Philip Allott recently recalled we have had four self-enlightenments of the European mind since the end of the Roman Empire in the West - the Carolingian renaissance of the 9th century, the 12th century renaissance centred on the University of Paris, the Italian renaissance of the 15th century and the 18th century Enlightenment.[254] This re-enlightenment process in Europe has occured at three century intervals which would mean that the next one is due in the first century of the next Millenium, beginning in 3 years time. With this backdrop, the challenge is to make sure that we indeed not only negotiate the 'footbridge to the Millenium' but that we develop new ideas that set in place the structures for organic growth for the longer time span. That is what will need to be translated into institutional terms in the early years of the third Millenium.

---

253. See, I. Ward, '(Pre)conceptions in European Law' 23 *Journal of Law and Society* (1996), p. 198.

254. See his erudite inaugural lecture at the ULB, Brussels: 'The Crisis of European Constitutionalism. Reflections on the Revolution in Europe', 25 March 1996.